365 PRODUCTIVITY SUTRAS

NIDHI M B
ANIL BRAHMANANDAN
K GOPALAKRISHNAN NAIR

INDIA • SINGAPORE • MALAYSIA

ISBN

Hardcase 979-8-88733-029-7
PaperBack 979-8-88733-027-3

PREFACE

Getting better results, or being more productive, is something that people strive to accomplish at work, around the house, or even in personal hobbies or activities. Productivity is a measure that evaluates the results in comparison to the inputs and efforts spared. The Asian Productivity Organization says that: *"Productivity is, above all, an attitude of mind. It seeks to continually improve what already exists. It is based on the belief that one can do things better today than yesterday and better tomorrow than today"*. People have been striving to balance output with the essential inputs since the beginning of time, so it's not surprising to find an overwhelming number of quotes in this topic. However these statements don't mean anything unless one is able to relate it to one's own experience and adapt the concept to improve oneself and the surroundings.

The premise that there is always scope for improvement or definitely a better way to do anything is very motivating and gives us hope. With this philosophy in mind, we've attempted to pen down a collection of statements related to different aspects of productivity applicable in a range of fields and circumstances. Our inspiration has been the words and thoughts of people who have been successful in different walks of life.

Whether you're looking for motivation to stay focused, set priorities, or simply get things done, here are 365 productivity sutras to keep you moving in the right direction. We hope productivity inspiration to be with the readers right from the day the book reaches their hands till the 365th day and continue to help them to be more productive!

We like to place on record our gratitude to the Notion Press team for the publication support. We place on record big thanks to Mr. G. Madhavan Nair, former chairman, ISRO who has taken pains to read through the content and was kind enough to write the foreword. We thank Respected Ganesh Ravi Pillai (Vice Chairman RP Group), Mr Shaun Sam Mathews (Project Engineer, The Boeing Company (USA)), and Ms Sujatha Singh (Productivity coach, International Coach Federation) for scripting the blurbs, Ms. Sukanya Srinivas for proof reading and Ms Jovita Asish for the cover page design. We thankfully acknowledge the support and cooperation of the family members of authors for making this work a reality.

Authors

FOREWORD

For any enterprise to succeed in the globalised economy the main contributors are quality, cost effectiveness and timely delivery. The economy is strongly dependent on agriculture, manufacturing and service sectors. Proper planning and implementation of all activities related to each sector is essential to achieve global standards. In order to achieve cost effectiveness the productivity must be maximised using available resources in an optimum manner. Most of the processes involve complex multidisciplinary activities and collaborative work involving men and machines. To improve the quality and productivity, assimilation of modern technology and upgrading of skills are essential. There are no shortcuts to success in an enterprise other than systematic planning and efficient implementation of the tasks within the shortest possible time. One of the key factors is the motivation and commitment of the team members.

This book aims to provide valuable suggestions on a day-to-day basis aiming at improving productivity in a systematic manner. The 365 sutras are postulated based on the knowledge and vast experience of three generations of academicians in the management field and their association with professional bodies such as Indian Institution of Industrial Engineering. It is not only the wisdom in the academic domain but also the observation from the field and corrective action implemented in the resolution of problems that has shaped the views expressed in this book.

Although the sutras are only brief statements they contain messages on good practices to be adopted in various segments like material supply, possess planning, quality control, skill development and timely product delivery. I am sure these principles can be implemented not only in the manufacturing sector but also on commercial activities and even on personal matters and managing one's own household. The book will be a good reference to professionals in the field.

I congratulate the authors Dr. K Gopalakrishnan Nair, Dr. B Anil, and Dr. M B Nidhi for their excellent team work. Incidentally they have a strong bond as Guru and Shishya as in Vedic literature. I wish good reading and best wishes for all their future ventures.

G Madhavan Nair
Former Chairman Indian Space research organisation

BEFORE YOU BEGIN

The 365 Productivity Sutras is a collection of observations and ideas related to productivity and its improvement. It includes informational, inspirational, motivational, directive and cautionary tips. As name implies there are 365 sutras as in the days of a year and are arranged in a sequential manner. One should read the sutras, understand the essence of it and try to relate with practical examples from knowledge or experience. One will get enriched and empowered to improve their productivity if this is practiced on a daily basis.

Wish you a great reading experience and success in the productivity journey.

Day 1

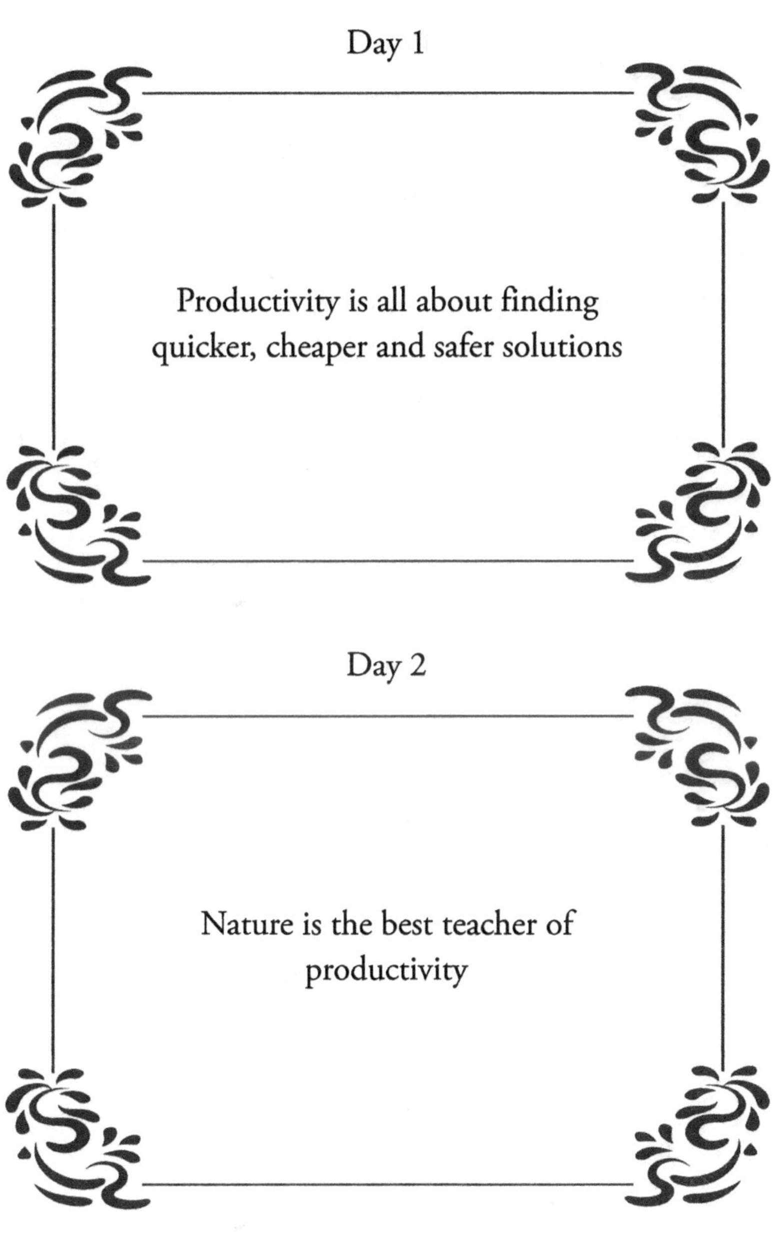

Productivity is all about finding quicker, cheaper and safer solutions

Day 2

Nature is the best teacher of productivity

Day 3

When people do more than what they are paid for, productivity gains

Day 4

A strong mind results in better productivity

Day 5

A healthy work-life balance nurtures productivity

Day 6

There is always a better and efficient way to do every chore

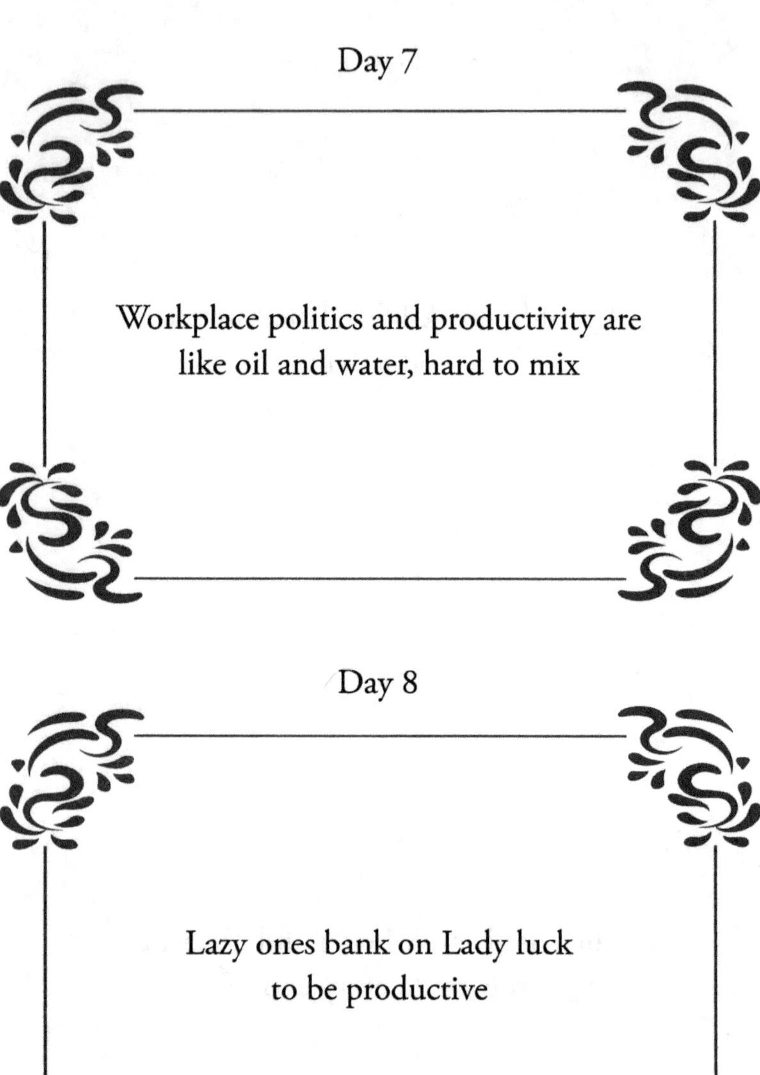

Day 7

Workplace politics and productivity are like oil and water, hard to mix

Day 8

Lazy ones bank on Lady luck to be productive

Day 9

Productivity embraces those who strive for excellence

Day 10

No self confidence,
No success in productivity

Day 11

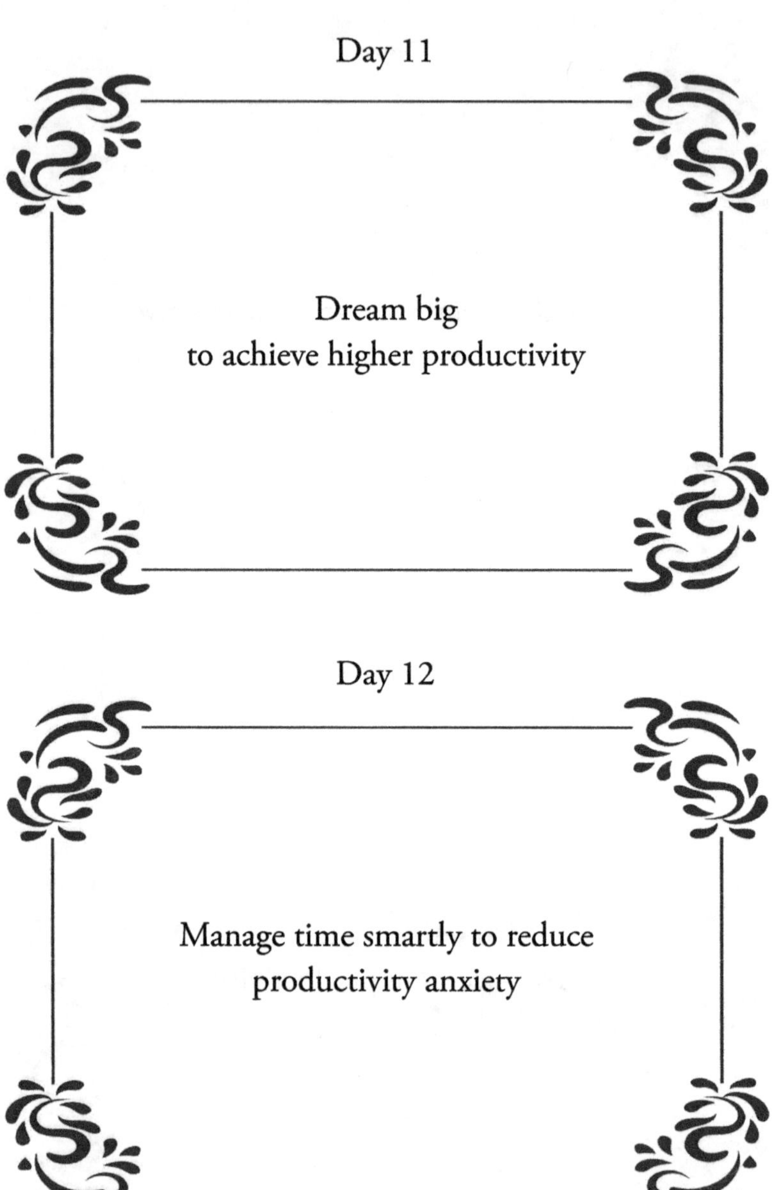

Dream big
to achieve higher productivity

Day 12

Manage time smartly to reduce productivity anxiety

Day 13

Being purposefully productive
is to excel

Day 14

Learning to be productive everyday is a
lifetime catalyst

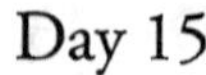

Day 15

Smart and steady work bring about productivity

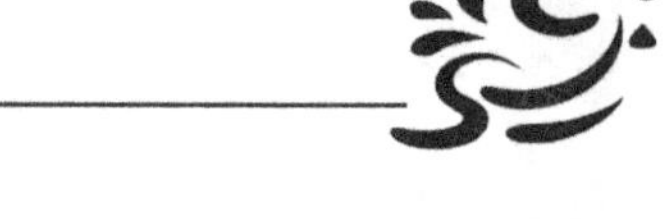

Day 16

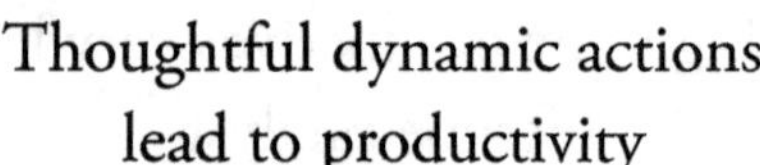

Thoughtful dynamic actions lead to productivity

Day 17

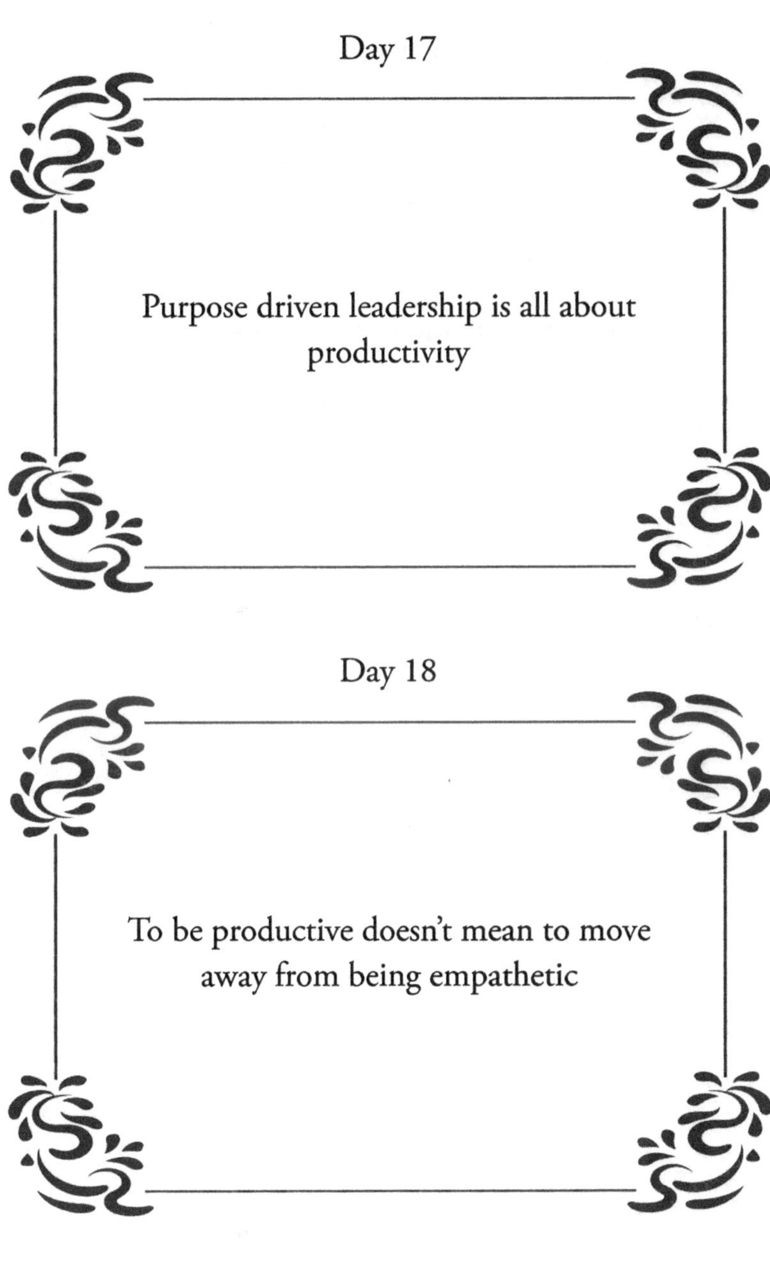

Purpose driven leadership is all about productivity

Day 18

To be productive doesn't mean to move away from being empathetic

Day 19

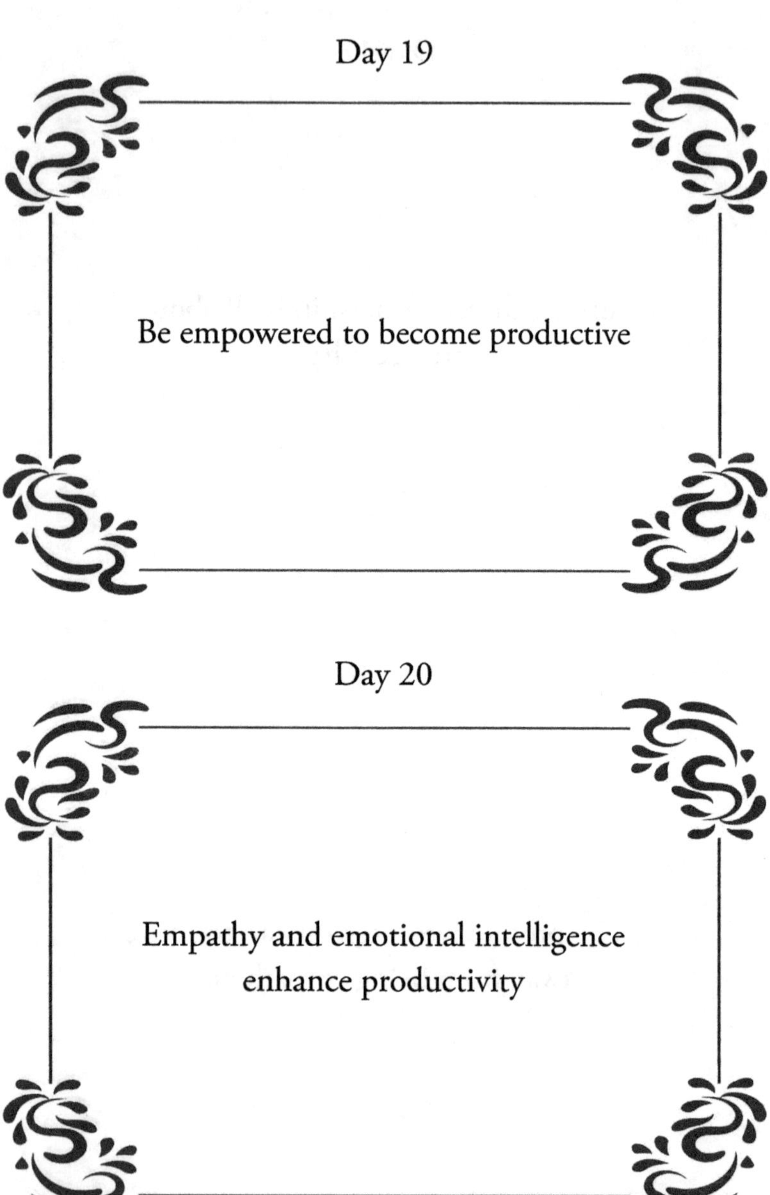

Be empowered to become productive

Day 20

Empathy and emotional intelligence enhance productivity

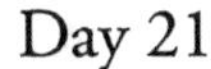

Day 21

One becomes what one dreams of,
hence dream to be productive

Day 22

The enigma of existence vanishes with
productive actions

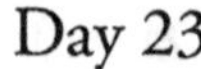

Day 23

Doing the best and leaving the rest
entails productive outcomes

Day 24

When right efforts are in place,
productivity follows

Day 25

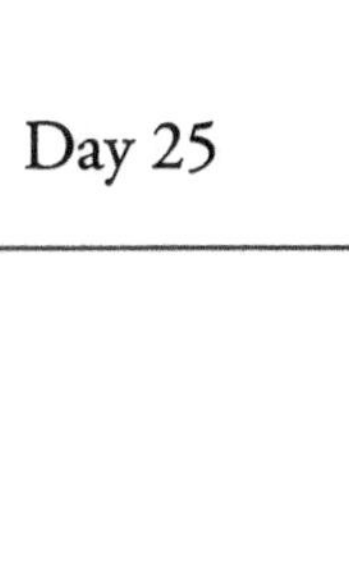

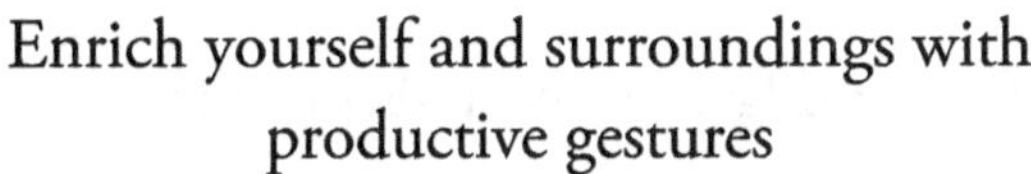

Enrich yourself and surroundings with productive gestures

Day 26

At times, doing nothing is also a productive engagement

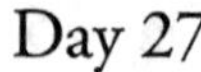

Day 27

Fear and laziness curtails productivity

Day 28

Sharing responsibilities and engaging all, is a sign of productivity

Day 29

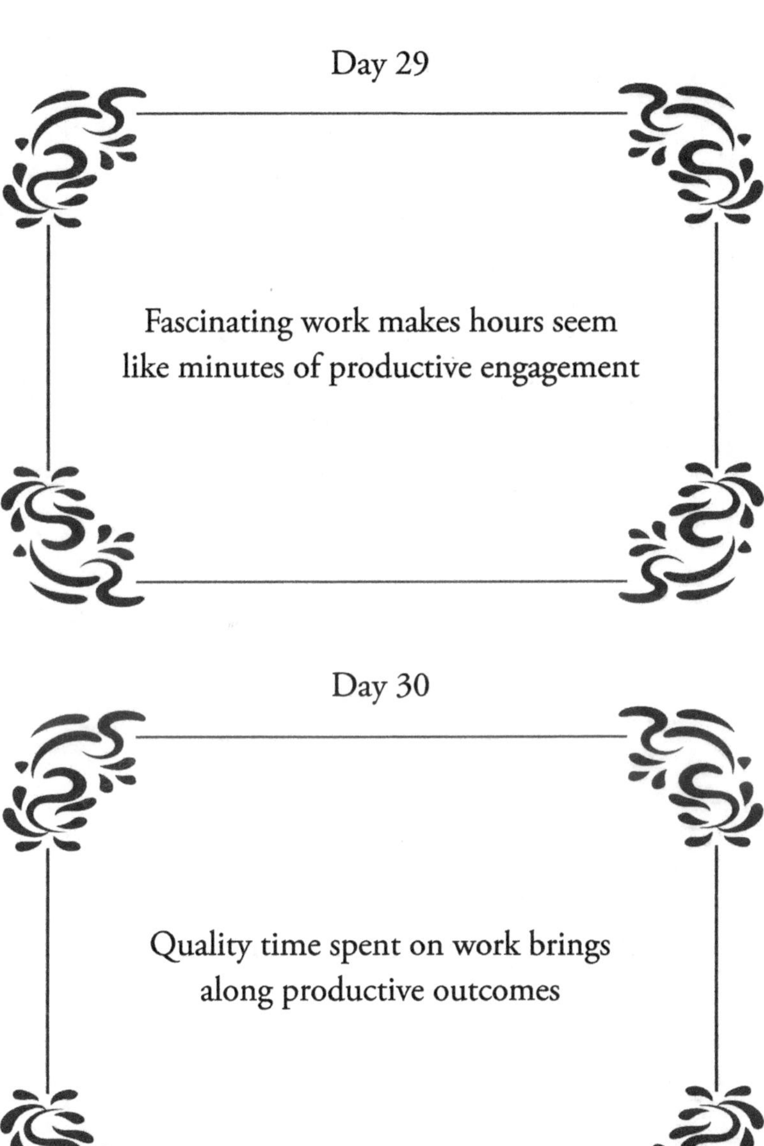

Fascinating work makes hours seem like minutes of productive engagement

Day 30

Quality time spent on work brings along productive outcomes

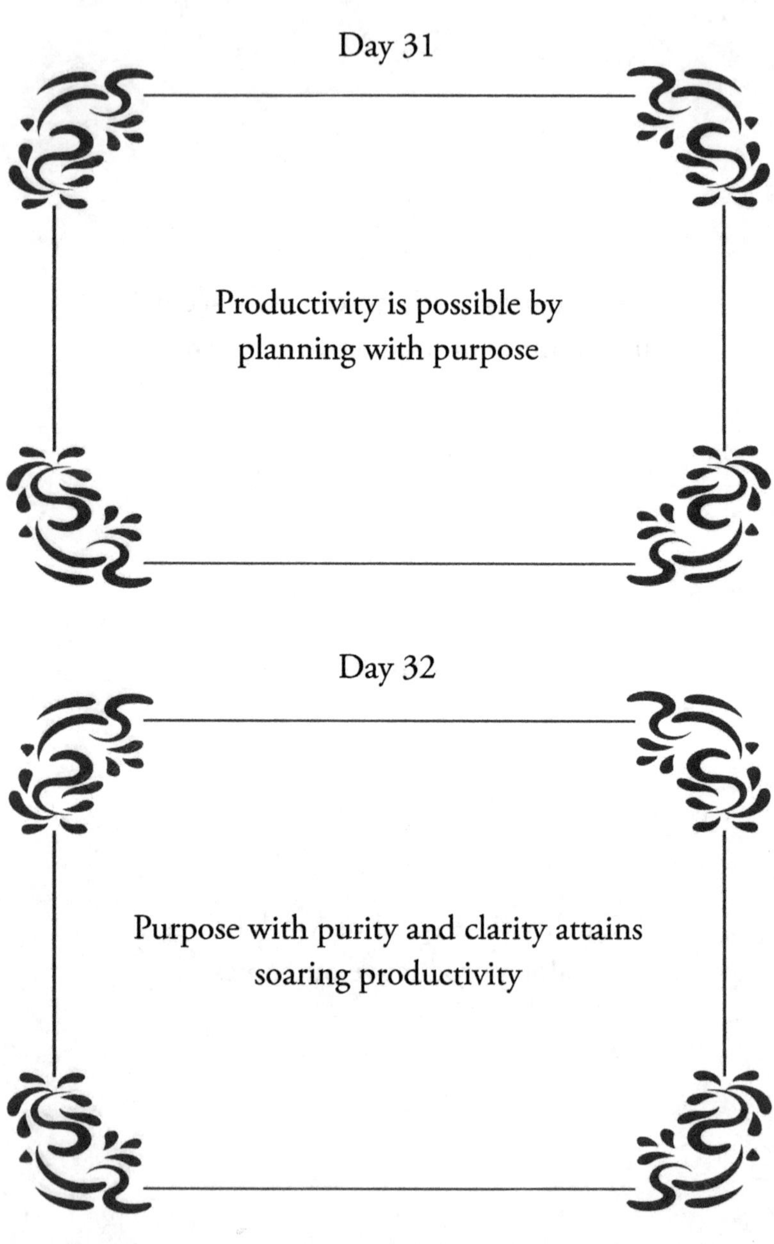

Day 31

Productivity is possible by planning with purpose

Day 32

Purpose with purity and clarity attains soaring productivity

Day 33

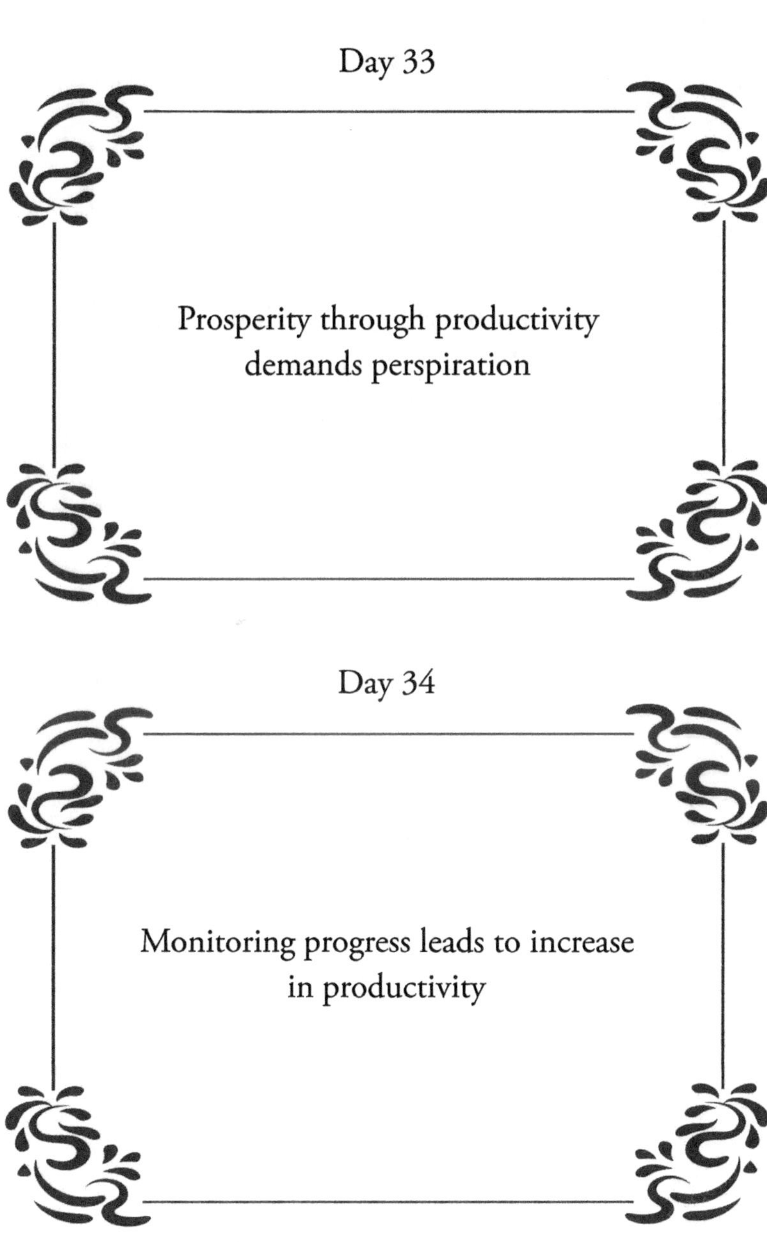

Prosperity through productivity demands perspiration

Day 34

Monitoring progress leads to increase in productivity

Day 35

Time spend on self glorification is time lost to productivity

Day 36

Being passionate about one's work fuels productivity

Day 37

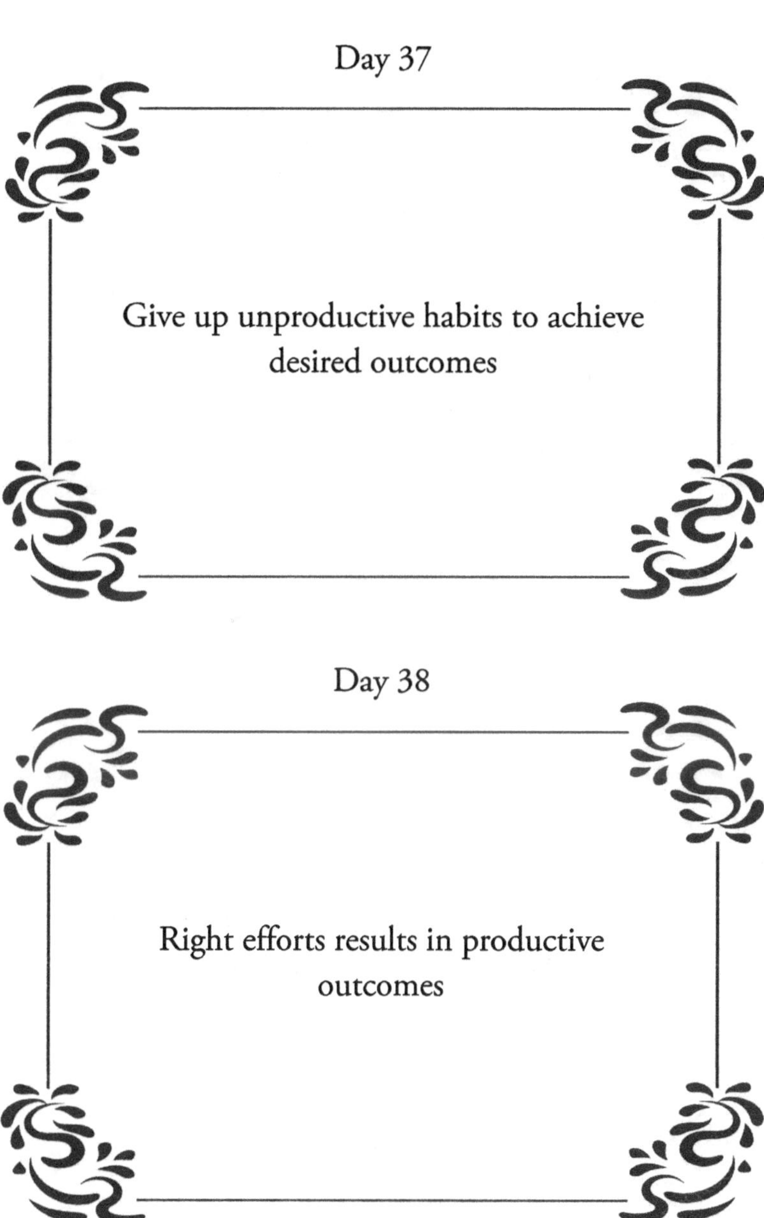

Give up unproductive habits to achieve desired outcomes

Day 38

Right efforts results in productive outcomes

Day 39

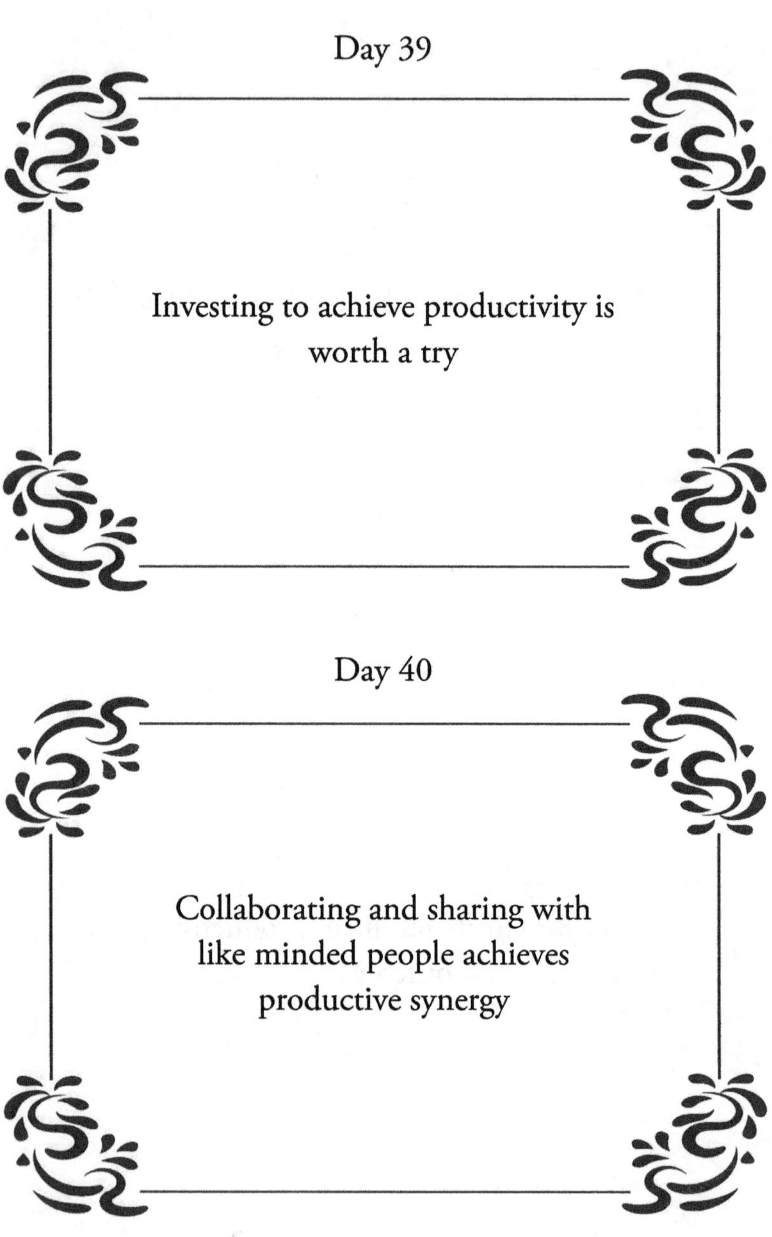

Investing to achieve productivity is worth a try

Day 40

Collaborating and sharing with like minded people achieves productive synergy

Day 41

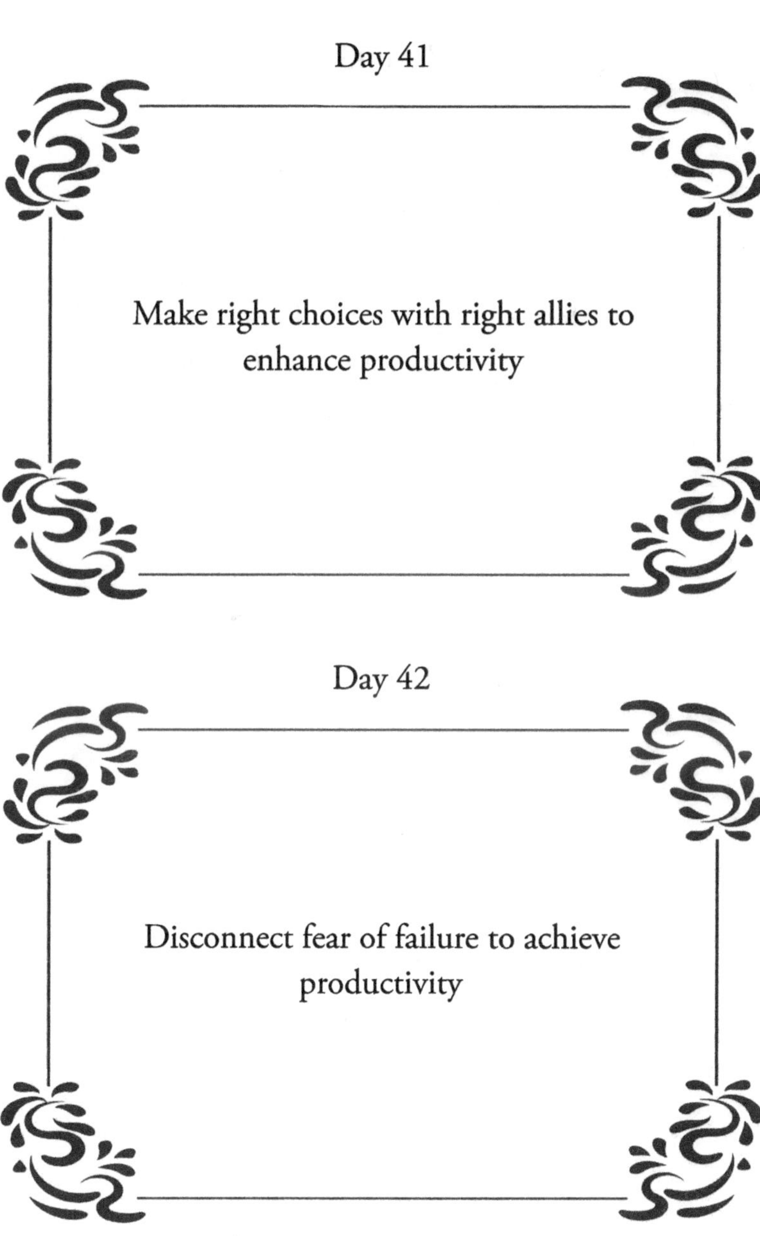

Make right choices with right allies to enhance productivity

Day 42

Disconnect fear of failure to achieve productivity

Day 43

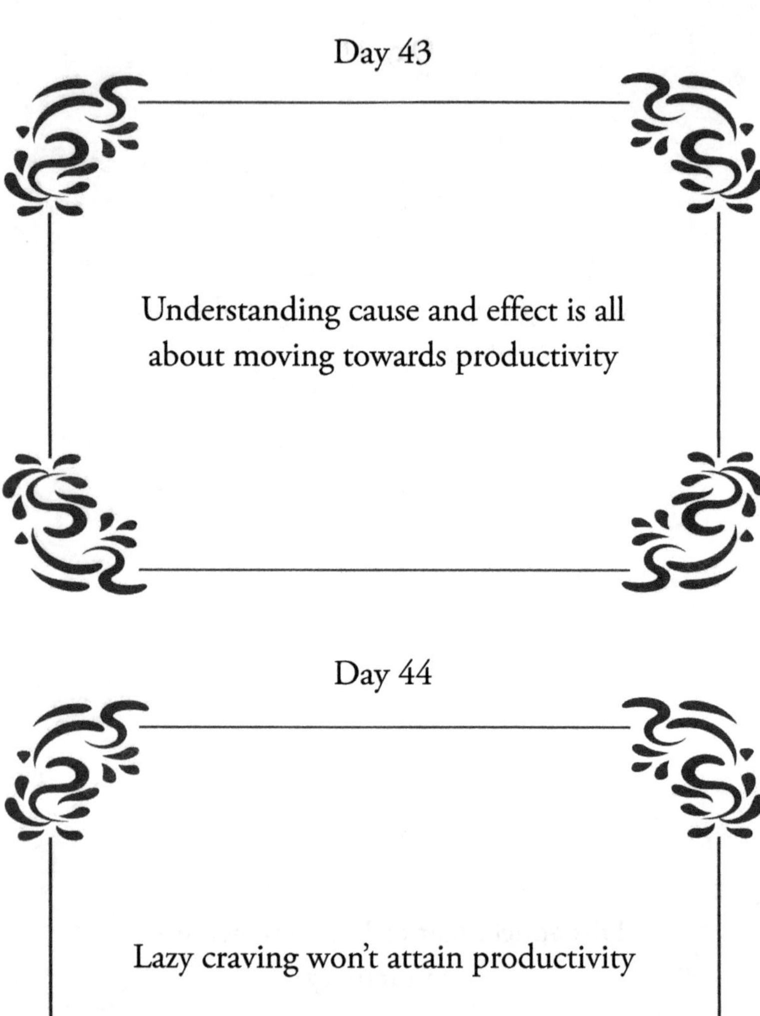

Understanding cause and effect is all about moving towards productivity

Day 44

Lazy craving won't attain productivity

Day 45

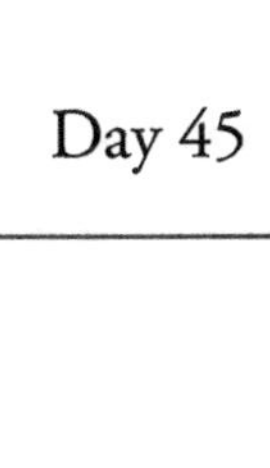

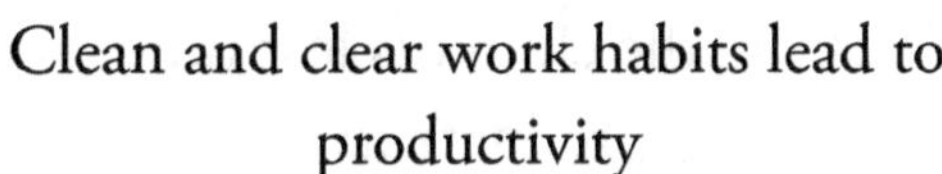

Clean and clear work habits lead to productivity

Day 46

Smooth like butter should be the productive engagement for best outcomes

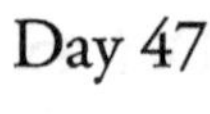

Day 47

Clearing the clutter is lost time for productivity

Day 48

Creative engagement leads to productive outcome

Day 49

The motto for productivity reads
"There is always room for improvement"

Day 50

Clarity of thoughts, speech and action
fetch productive outcomes

Day 51

Chasing comfort zones make one allergic to productivity

Day 52

Productivity results from commitment and cheerfulness

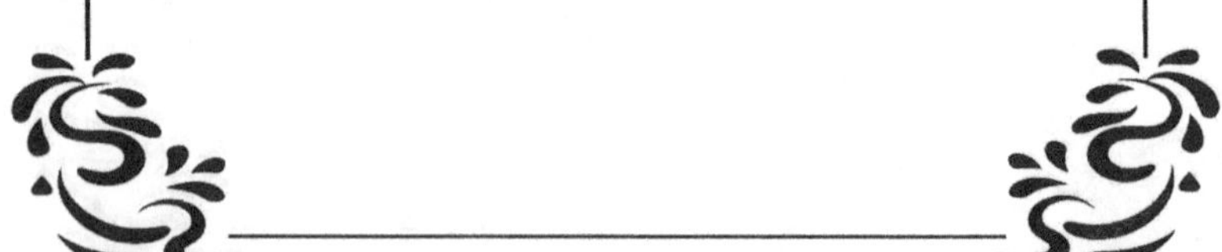

Day 53

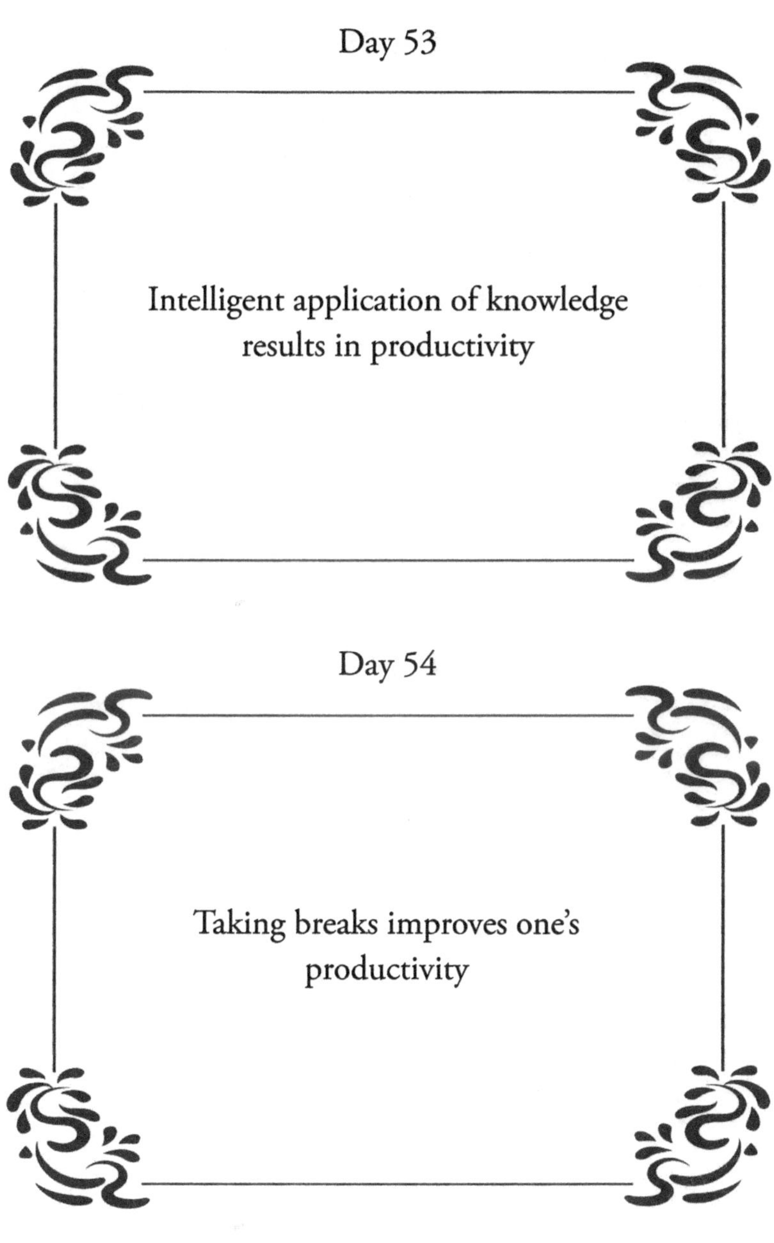

Intelligent application of knowledge results in productivity

Day 54

Taking breaks improves one's productivity

Day 55

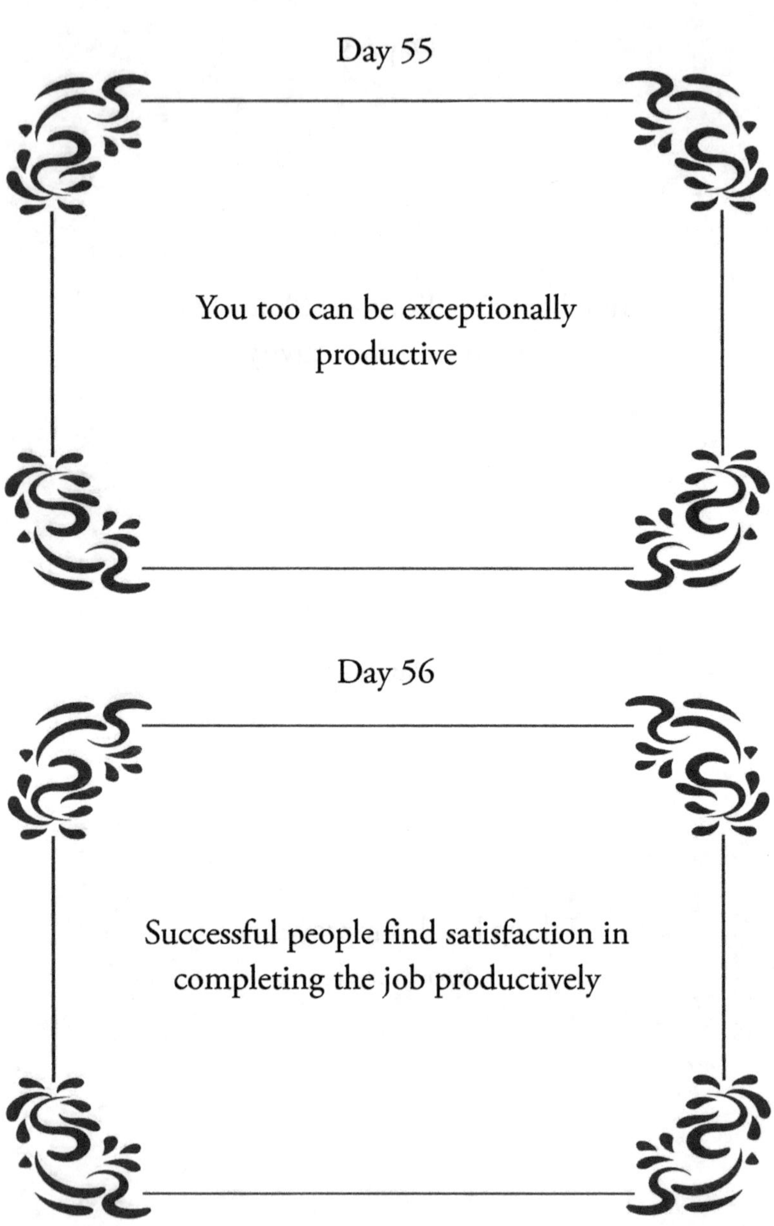

You too can be exceptionally productive

Day 56

Successful people find satisfaction in completing the job productively

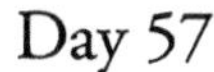

Day 57

Now is preferred than soon to achieve higher productivity

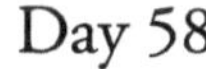

Day 58

Productivity prefers continuous improvement than perfection

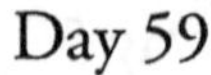

Day 59

Practice makes one skilled to become productive

Day 60

Measure productivity to improve it

Day 61

One must love one's own work to increase productivity

Day 62

Identify and eliminate inefficiencies to improve productivity

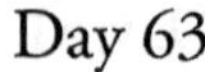

Day 63

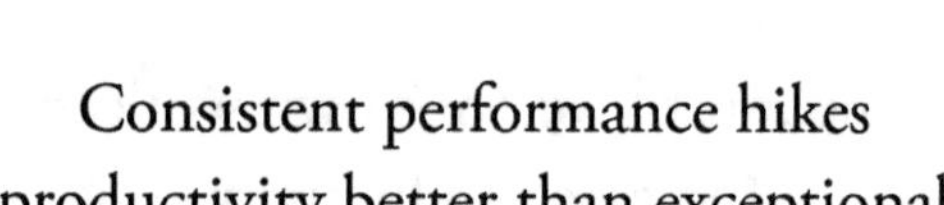

Consistent performance hikes productivity better than exceptional

Day 64

Setting attainable goals is important to engage productively

Day 65

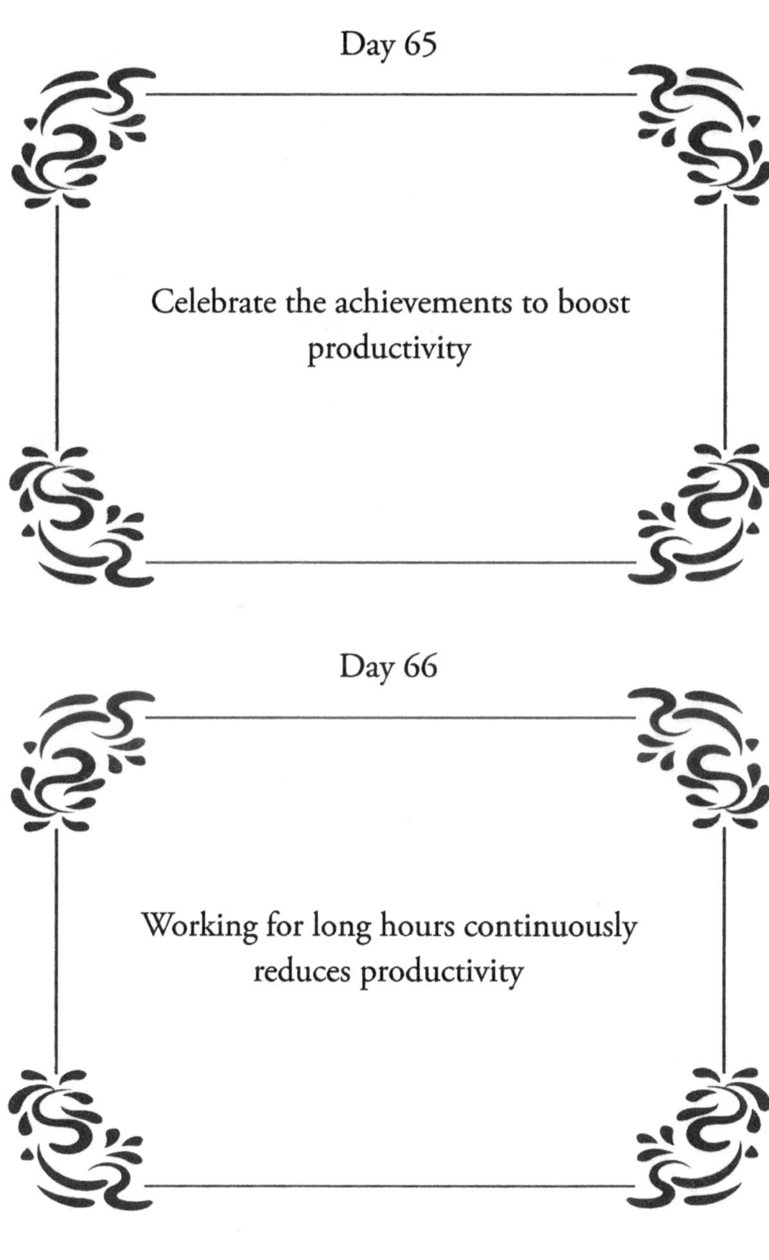

Celebrate the achievements to boost productivity

Day 66

Working for long hours continuously reduces productivity

Day 67

Lose attention, lose productivity

Day 68

Being fit is the key to good performance

Day 69

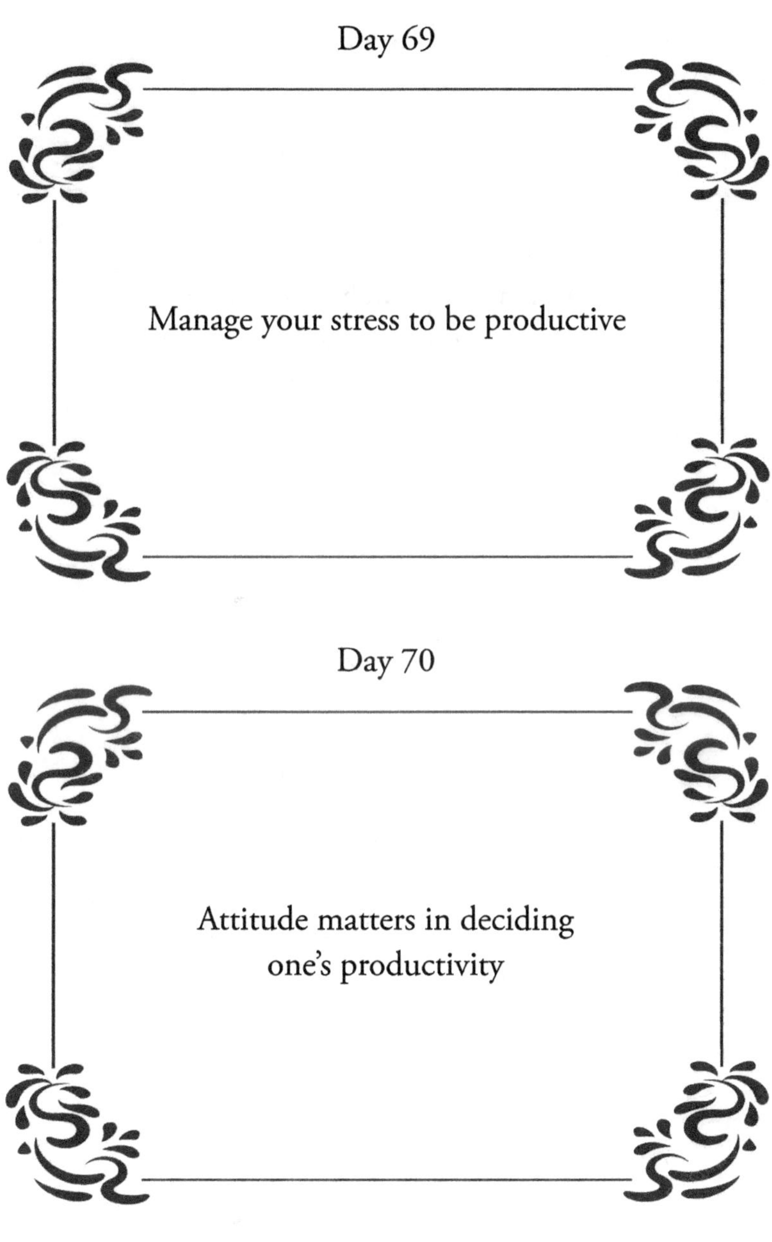

Manage your stress to be productive

Day 70

Attitude matters in deciding one's productivity

Day 71

Dress appropriately to become productive

Day 72

Why not try a walking meeting to charge up for productivity

Day 73

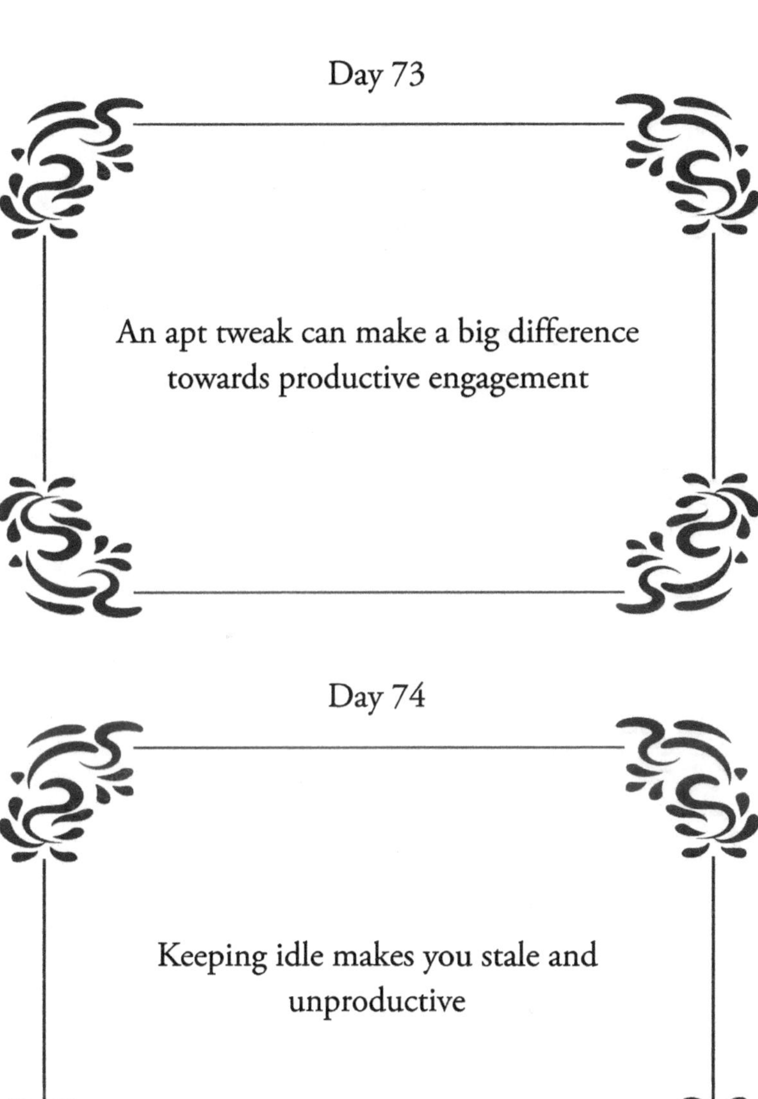

An apt tweak can make a big difference towards productive engagement

Day 74

Keeping idle makes you stale and unproductive

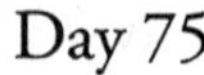

Day 75

'Do it right first time every time'
leads to higher productivity

Day 76

Too much documentation leaves no
room for productive work

Day 77

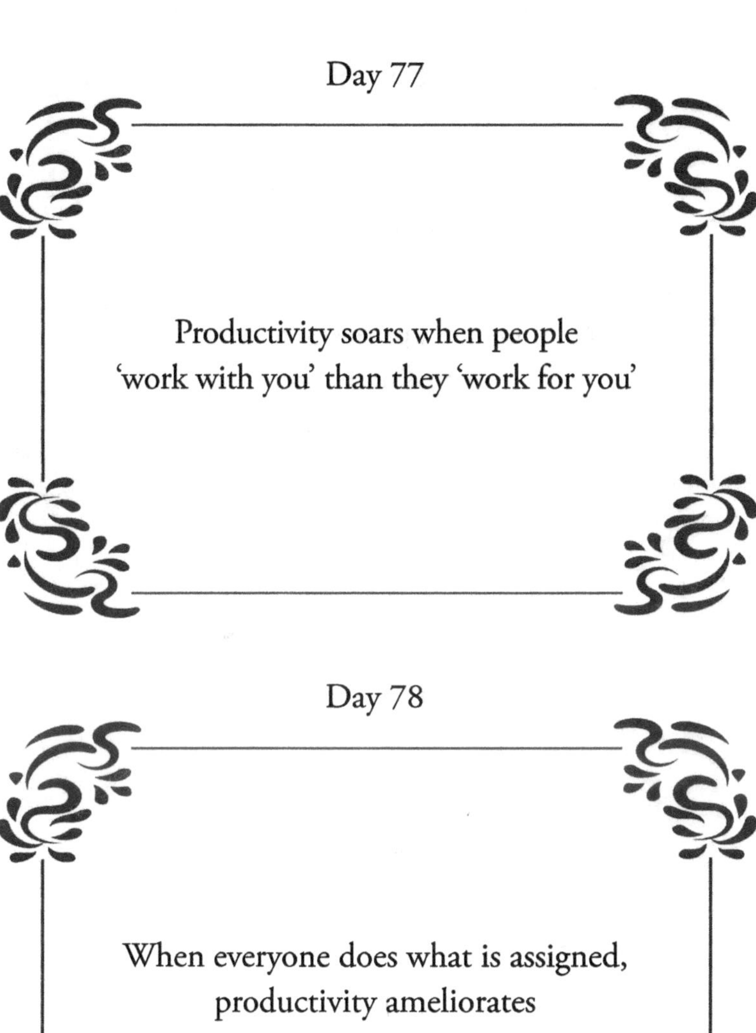

Productivity soars when people
'work with you' than they 'work for you'

Day 78

When everyone does what is assigned,
productivity ameliorates

Day 79

Mothers are our best teachers on productivity

Day 80

'Focus on work when on work' for best productivity

Day 81

Hard work never hurts when productivity is the goal

Day 82

To be productive, learn to shoulder responsibilities

Day 83

Challenges make you stronger to become productive

Day 84

One cannot be master of all trades but productive in some

Day 85

Know your limitations to tackle them better to become productive

Day 86

Never expect free meals when one's aim is to be highly productive

Day 87

The secret to becoming a
productivity champion is
good planning, preparation, execution
and consistent follow up

Day 88

Unless one attempts, one can't
accomplish high productivity

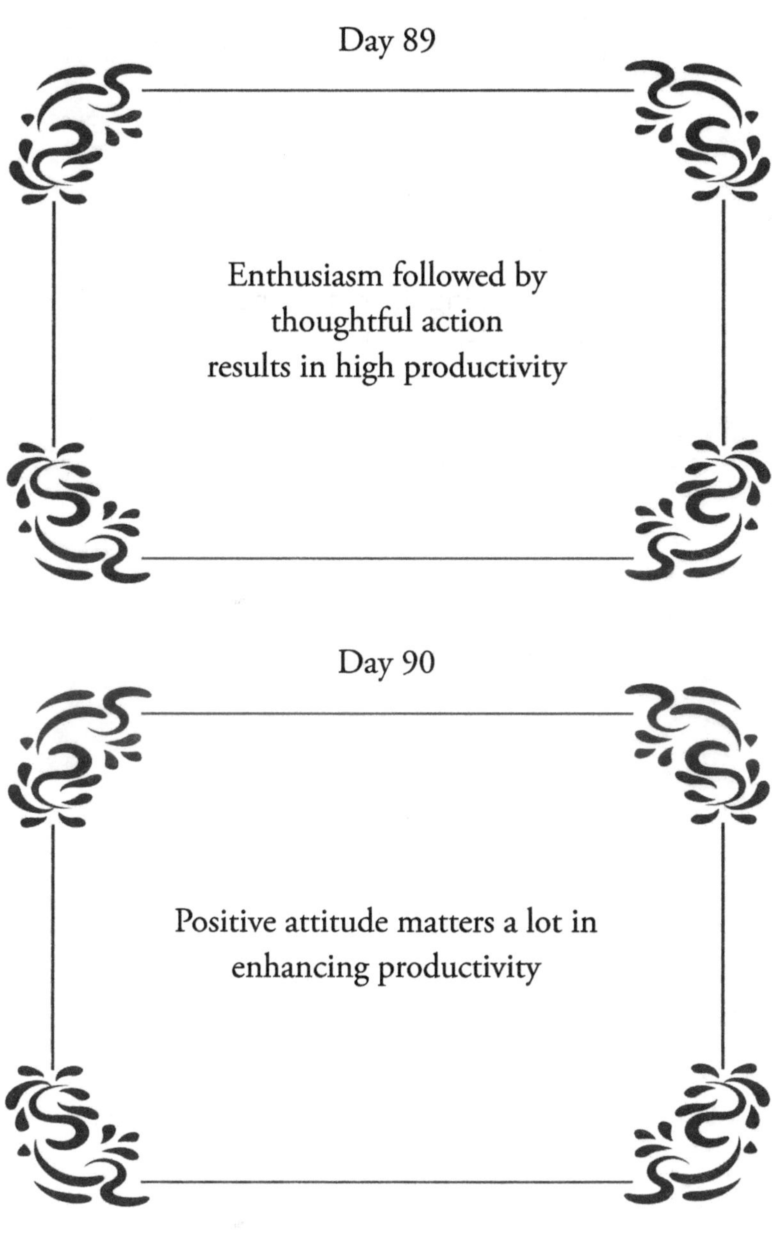

Day 89

Enthusiasm followed by
thoughtful action
results in high productivity

Day 90

Positive attitude matters a lot in
enhancing productivity

Day 91

Sharpening the tools is not a waste of time to be productive

Day 92

Productivity is to be judged by the results not by flaunt

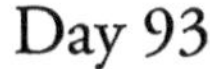

Day 93

Knowledge on productivity is worthless without implementation

Day 94

Start the productivity journey with determination to end with satisfaction

Day 95

Deeds speak better than words
in productivity

Day 96

One's actions define
how productive one is

Day 97

Creative ideas are the raw material to augment productivity

Day 98

Follow up motivates the lethargic ones to become productive

Day 99

For higher productivity, don't wait till tomorrow to act

Day 100

Until one dares, productivity looks invincible

Day 101

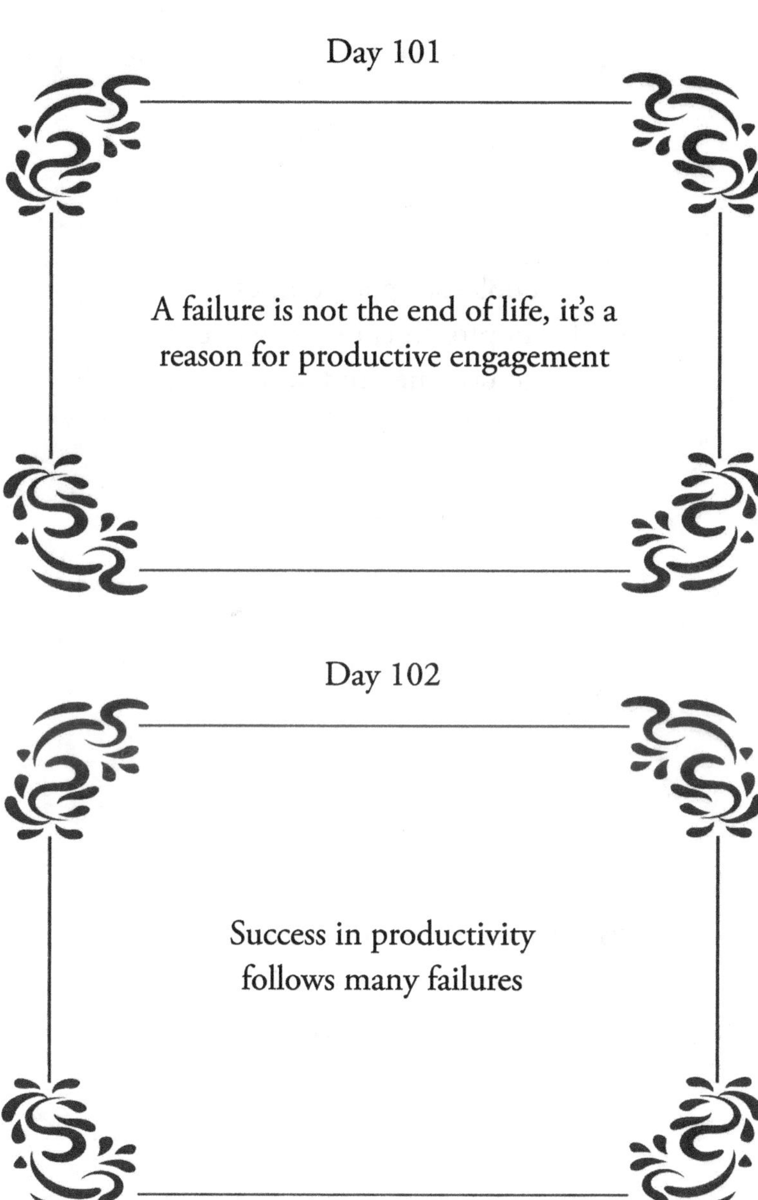

A failure is not the end of life, it's a reason for productive engagement

Day 102

Success in productivity follows many failures

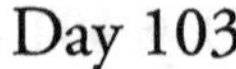

Day 103

Look for opportunities
for improvement everywhere
to become productive

Day 104

Be in the comfort zone and remain
mediocre in productivity

Day 105

Productivity enhancement don't happen on its own

Day 106

Knee-jerk reactions don't help improve productivity

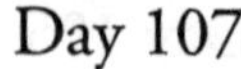

Day 107

Try to see the big picture to engage productively

Day 108

Without problems there is no reason to strive for higher productivity

Day 109

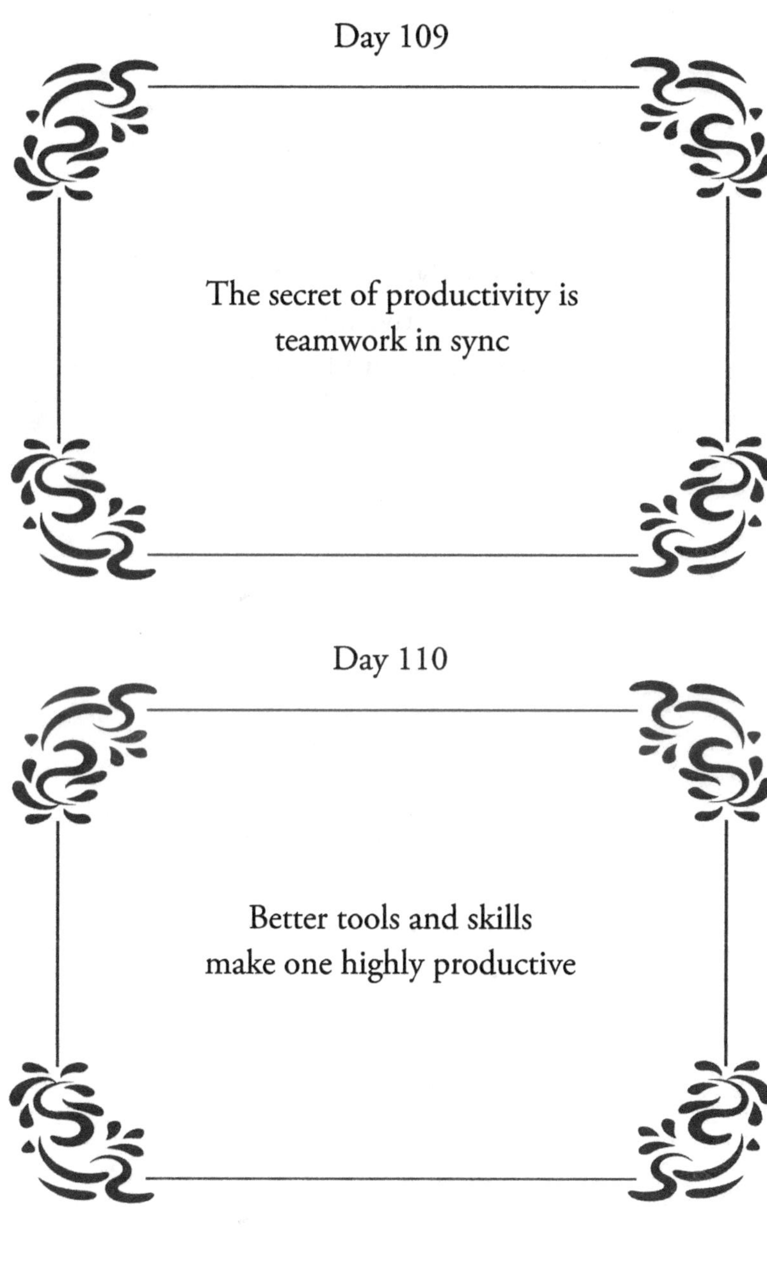

The secret of productivity is
teamwork in sync

Day 110

Better tools and skills
make one highly productive

Day 111

Productivity advocates
to strive for
more output with less input

Day 112

Higher the productivity,
longer the leisure time

Day 113

For higher productivity,
do the tough jobs when you are fittest

Day 114

Prepare a To-Do list every time to
increase productivity

Day 115

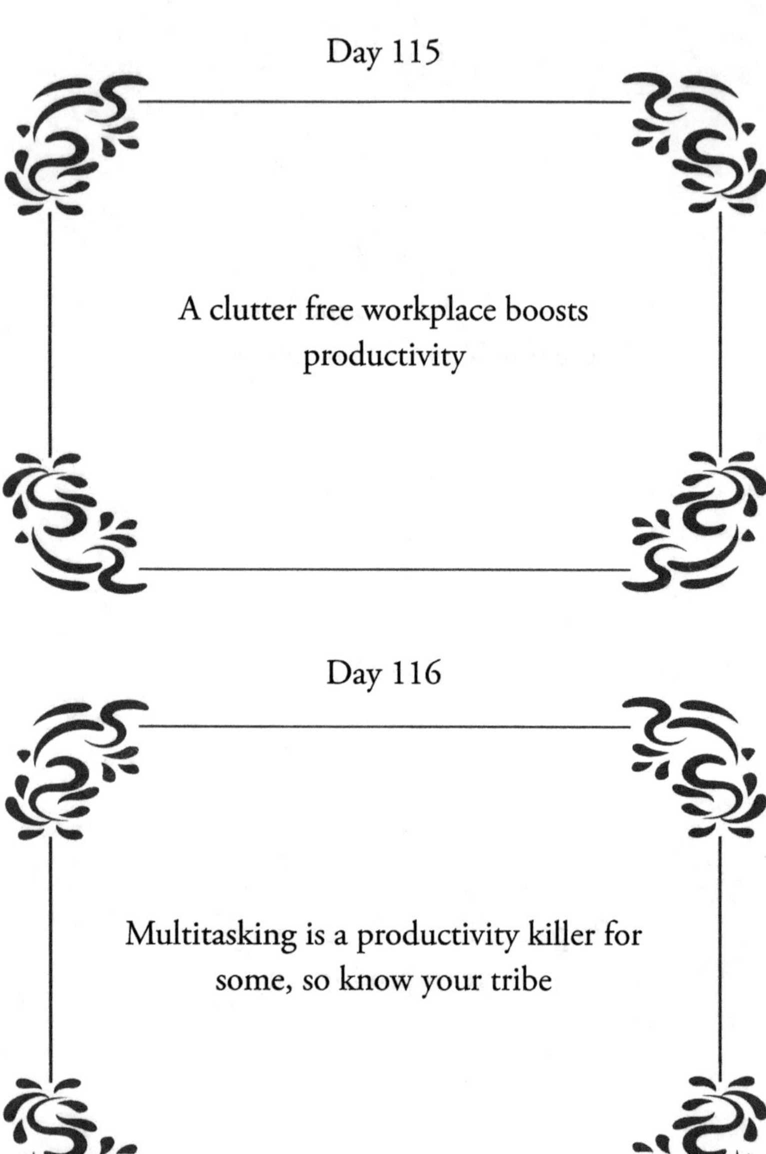

A clutter free workplace boosts productivity

Day 116

Multitasking is a productivity killer for some, so know your tribe

Day 117

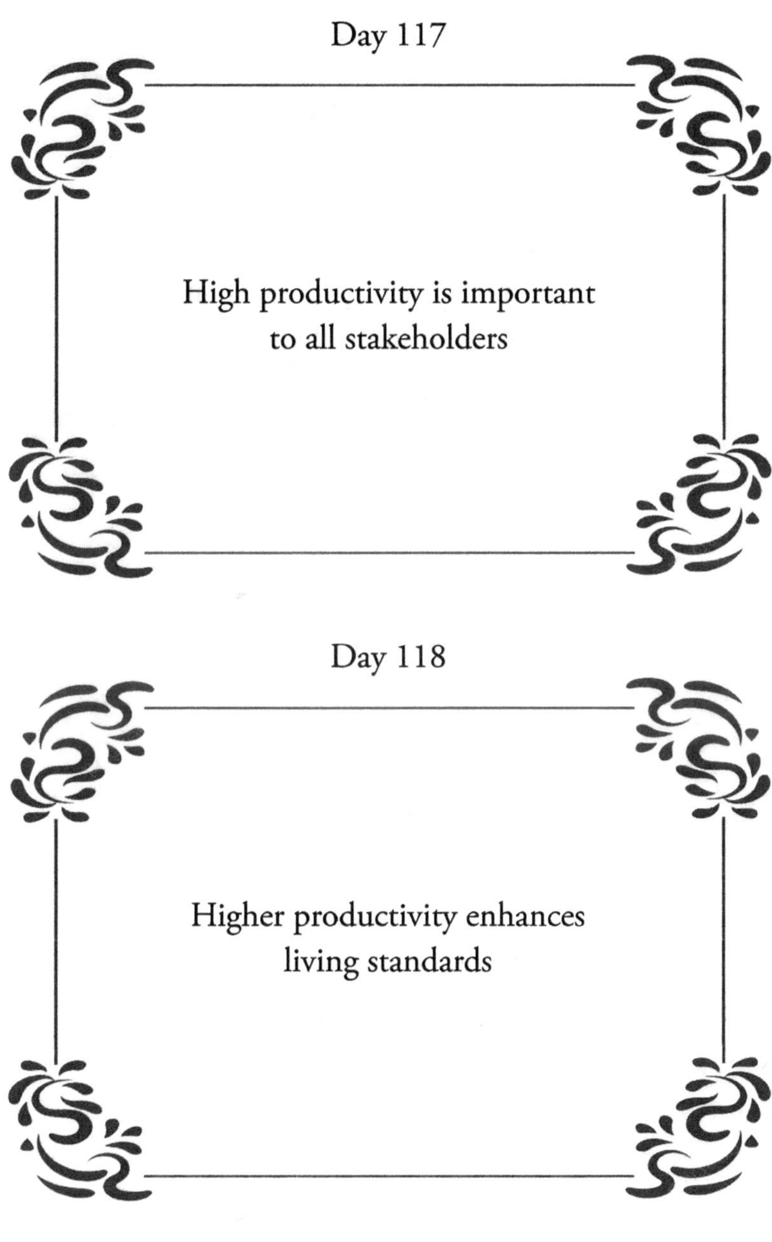

High productivity is important
to all stakeholders

Day 118

Higher productivity enhances
living standards

Day 119

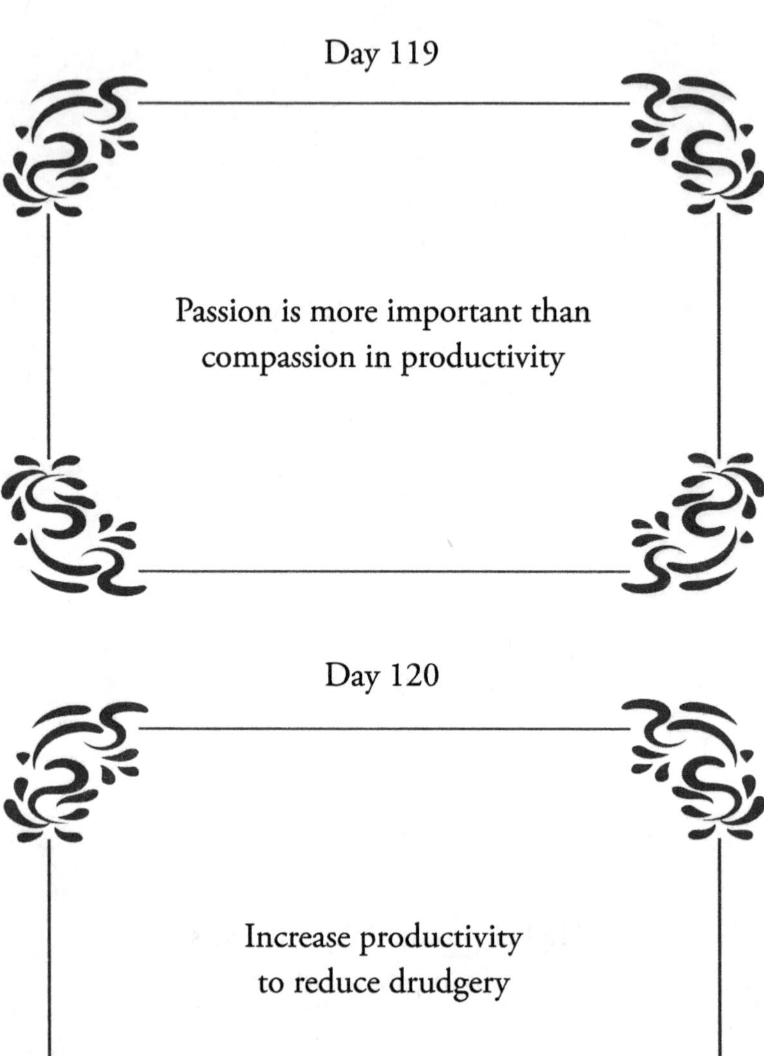

Passion is more important than compassion in productivity

Day 120

Increase productivity to reduce drudgery

Day 121

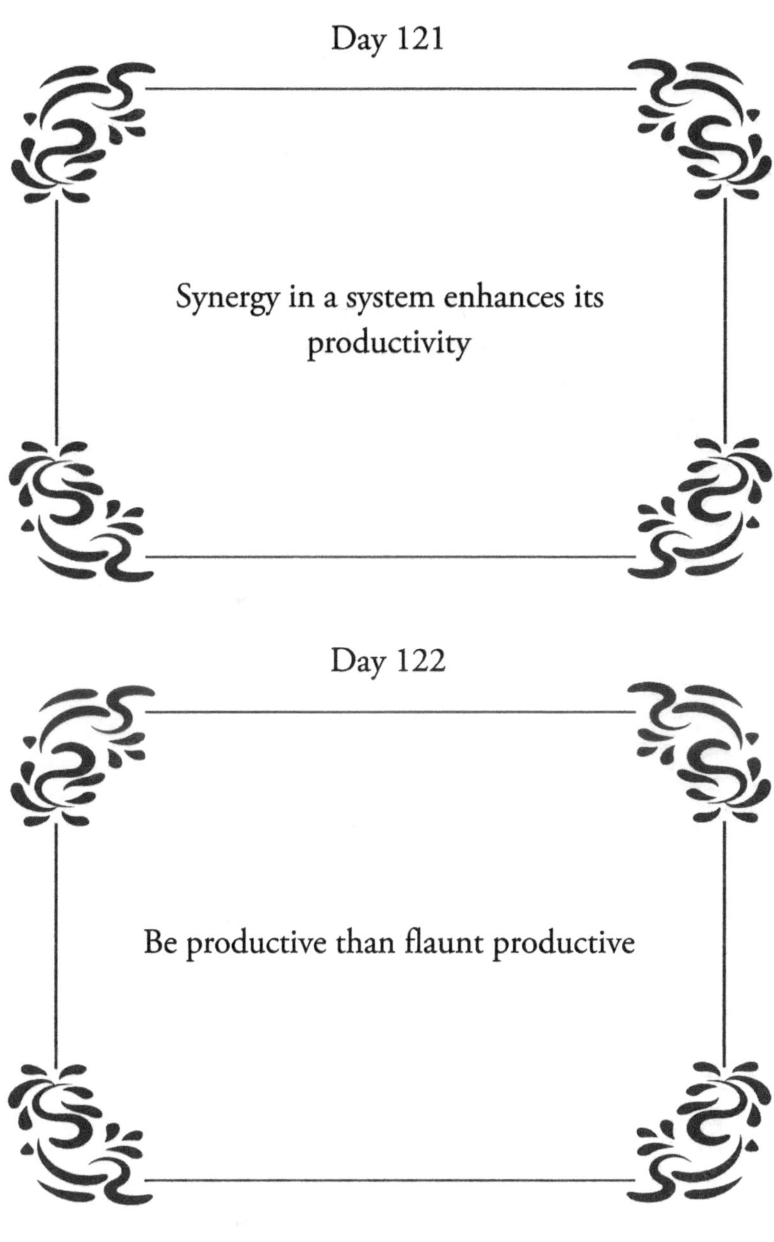

Synergy in a system enhances its productivity

Day 122

Be productive than flaunt productive

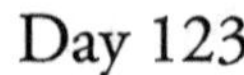

Day 123

When we place quality in front,
productivity follows

Day 124

Give wings to your imagination to
reach productivity goals

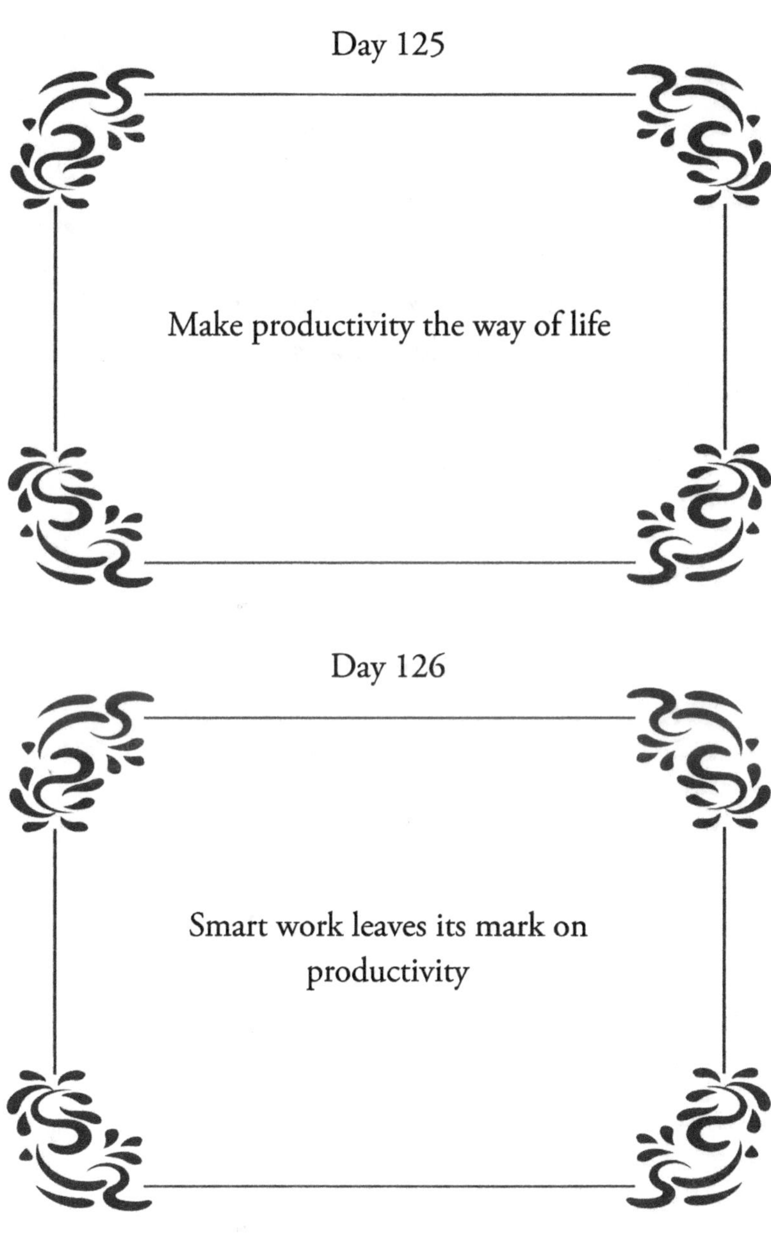

Day 125

Make productivity the way of life

Day 126

Smart work leaves its mark on productivity

Day 127

Practice prepares one for
productive acts

Day 128

Don't worry about mistakes,
it offer opportunity to learn

Day 129

To achieve higher productivity, never neglect details

Day 130

To become productive, be vigilant and watch for the signals

Day 131

Innovation leads to higher productivity

Day 132

Knowing what to do will not increase productivity, doing it will

Day 133

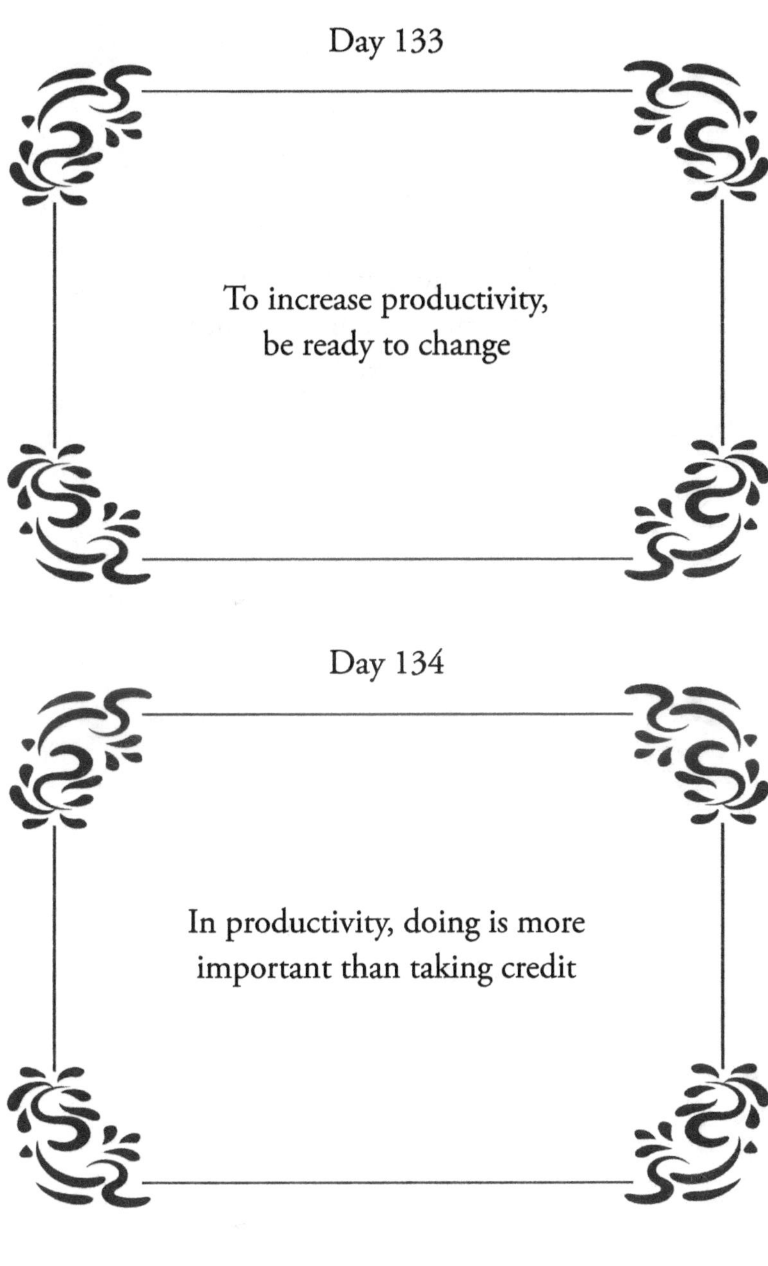

To increase productivity,
be ready to change

Day 134

In productivity, doing is more important than taking credit

Day 135

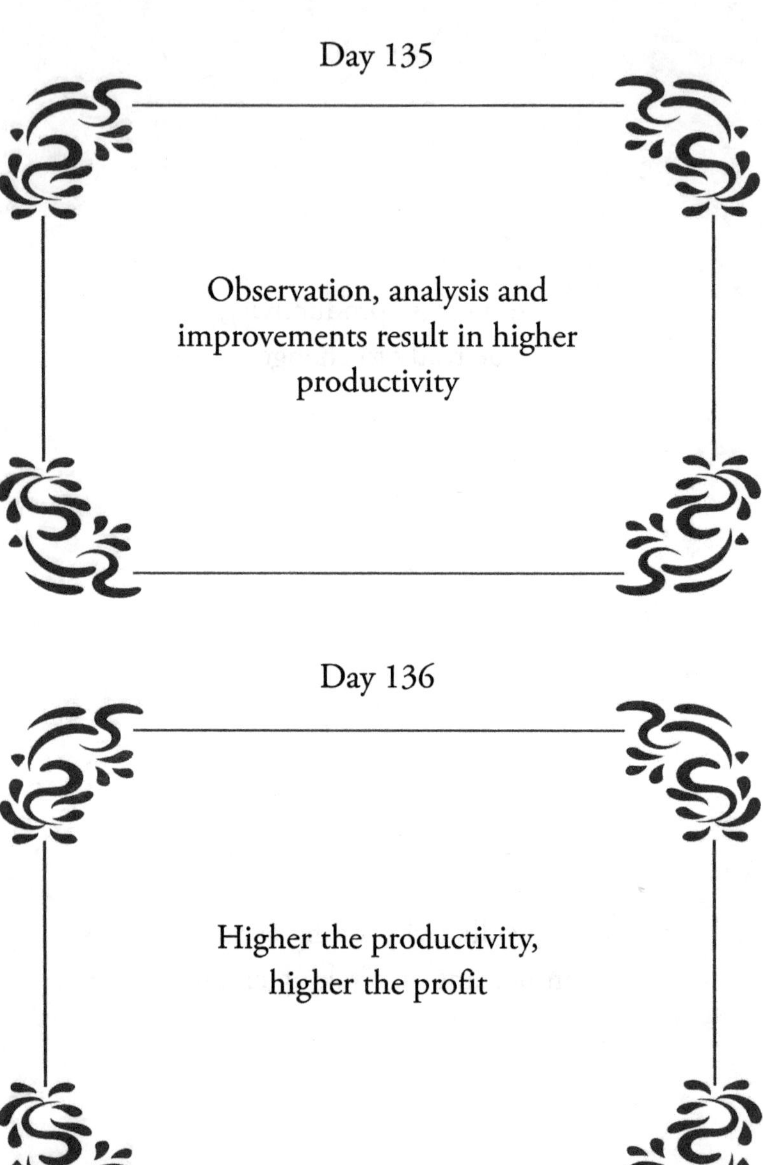

Observation, analysis and improvements result in higher productivity

Day 136

Higher the productivity, higher the profit

Day 137

Maintaining good relationships promote productivity

Day 138

In a team, alignment of thoughts helps achieve higher productivity

Day 139

Productivity follows those who are passionate about work

Day 140

Success will definitely follow productive actions

Day 141

Productivity
is everyone's responsibility

Day 142

Now is the right time to act to achieve higher productivity

Day 143

Every act matters in the journey towards higher productivity

Day 144

Productivity is the solution, not a problem

Day 145

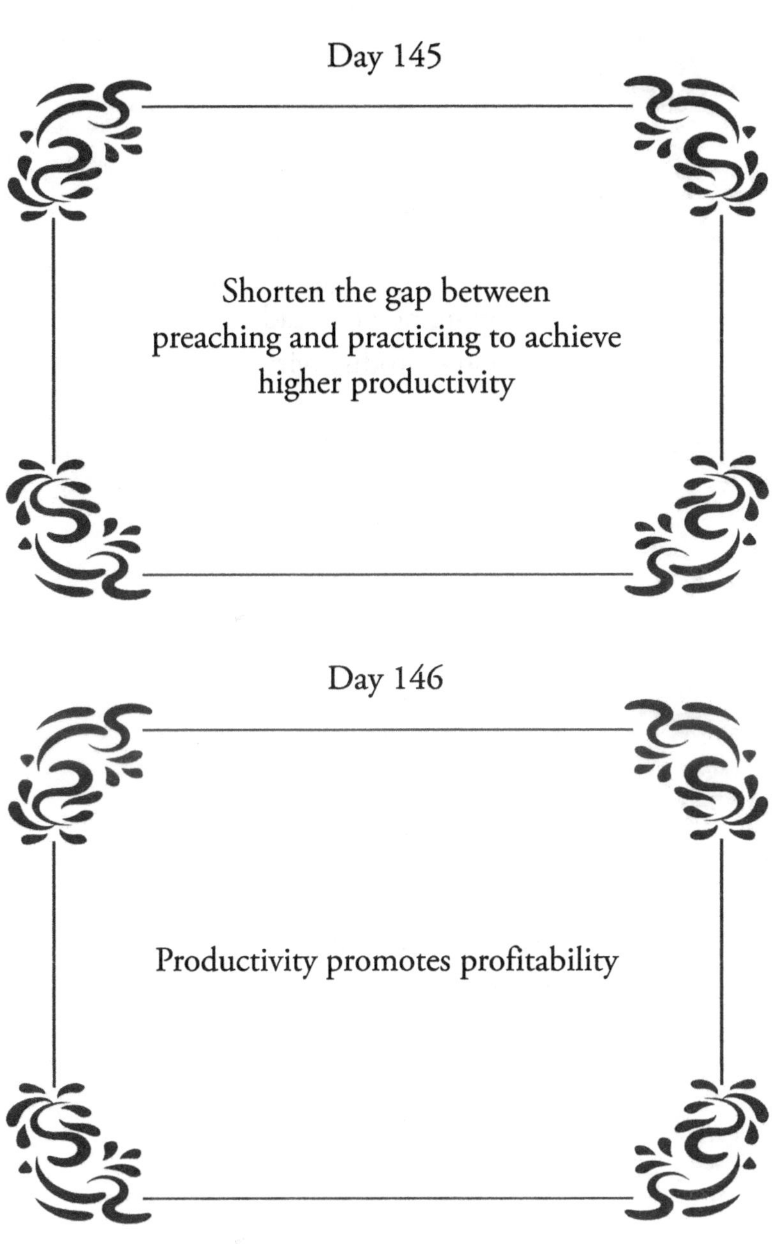

Shorten the gap between preaching and practicing to achieve higher productivity

Day 146

Productivity promotes profitability

Day 147

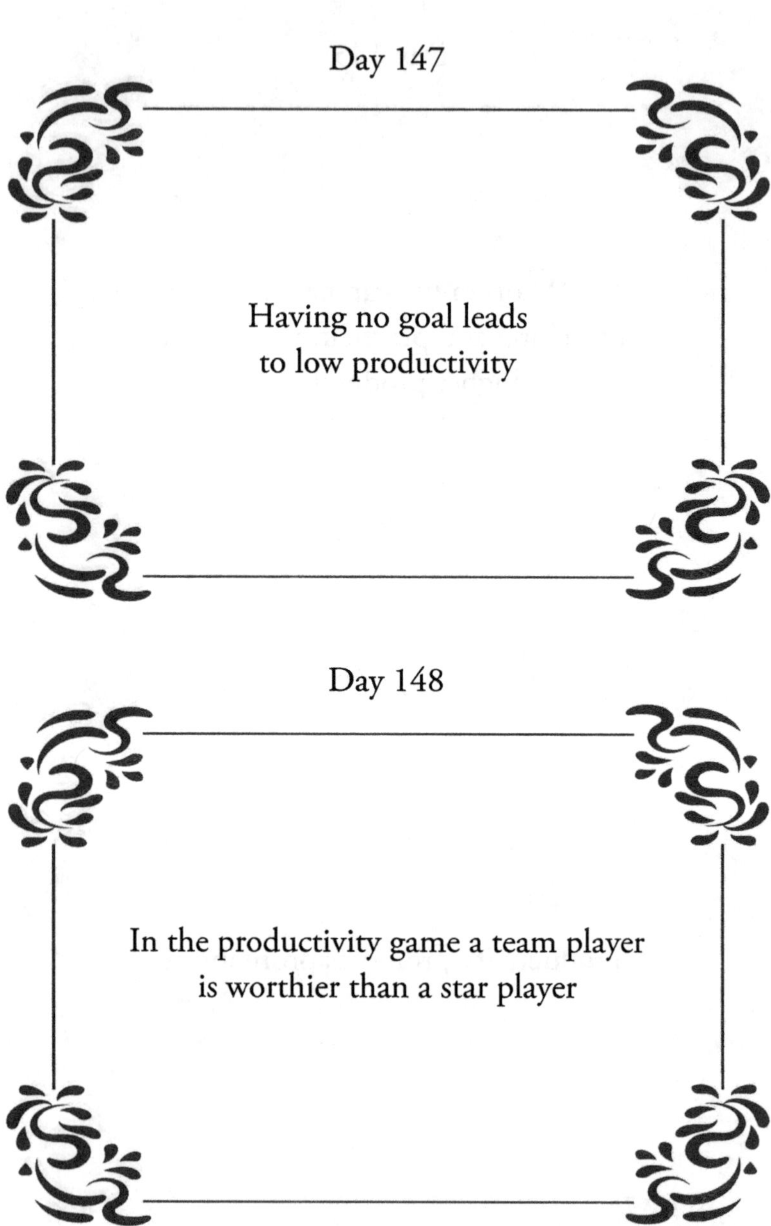

Having no goal leads
to low productivity

Day 148

In the productivity game a team player
is worthier than a star player

Day 149

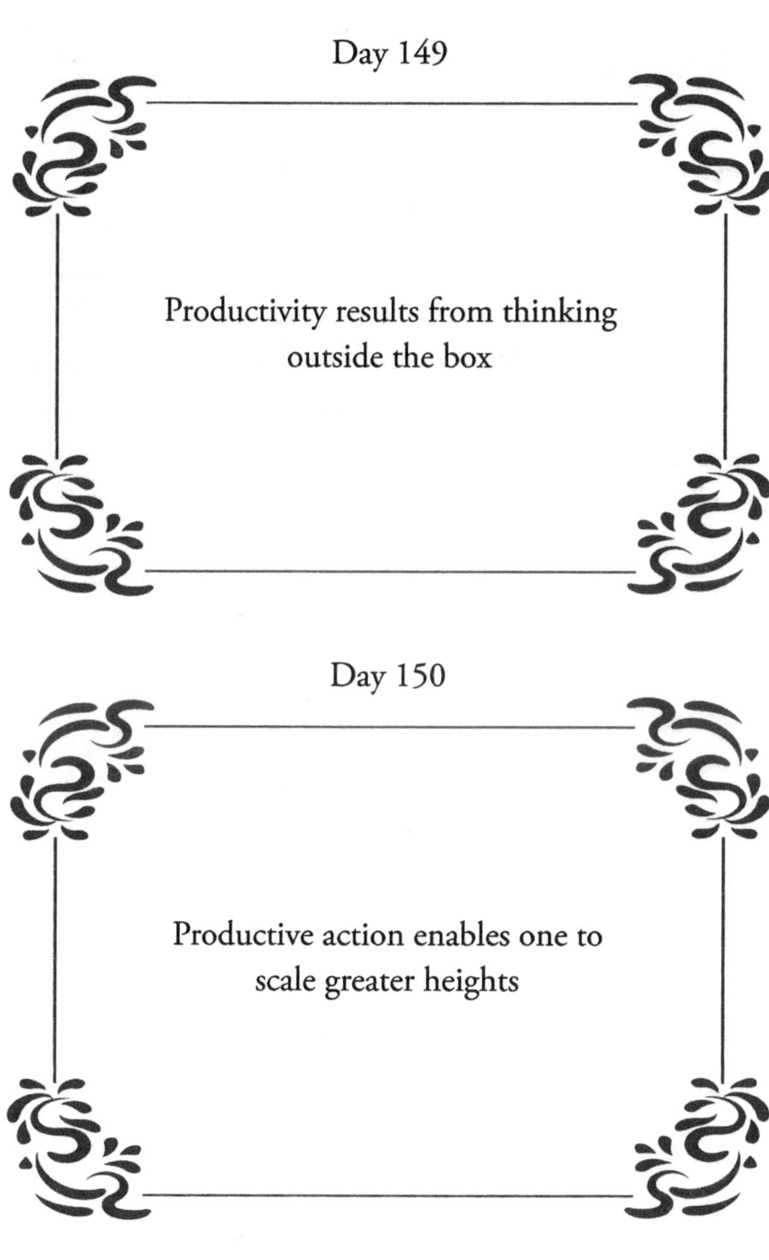

Productivity results from thinking outside the box

Day 150

Productive action enables one to scale greater heights

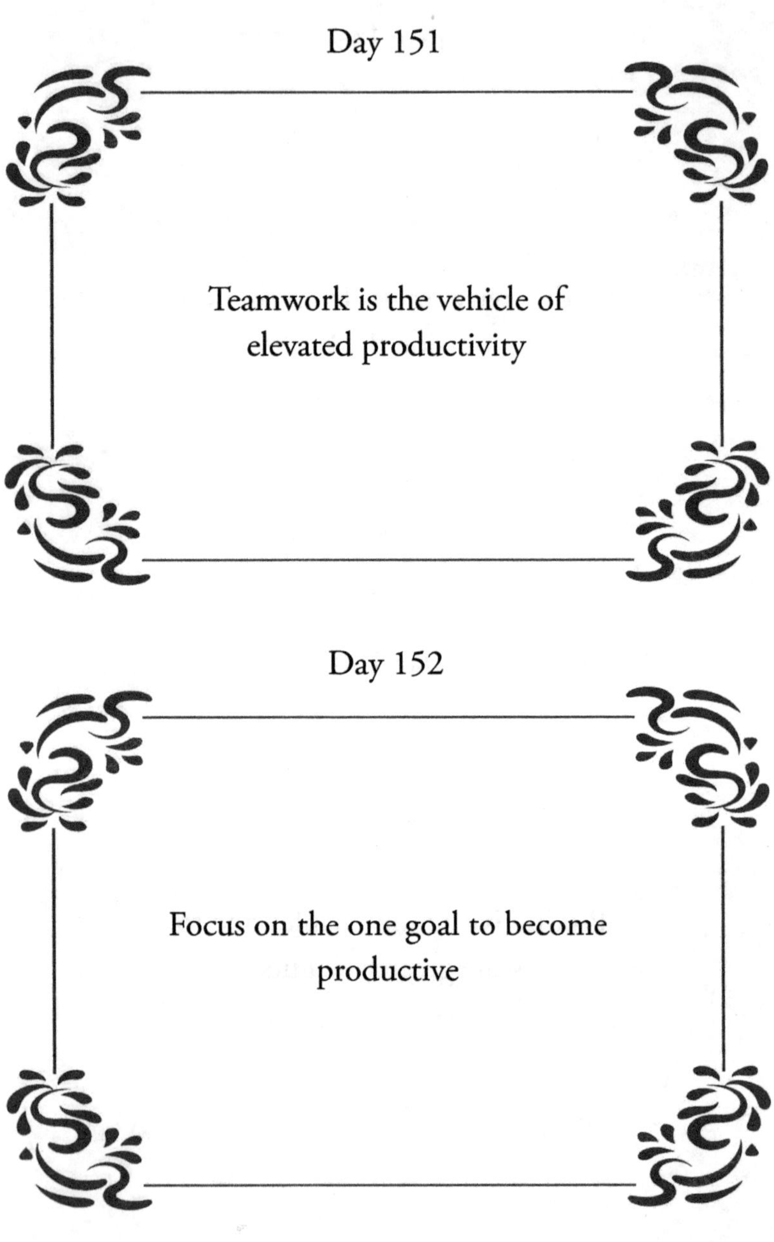

Day 151

Teamwork is the vehicle of elevated productivity

Day 152

Focus on the one goal to become productive

Day 153

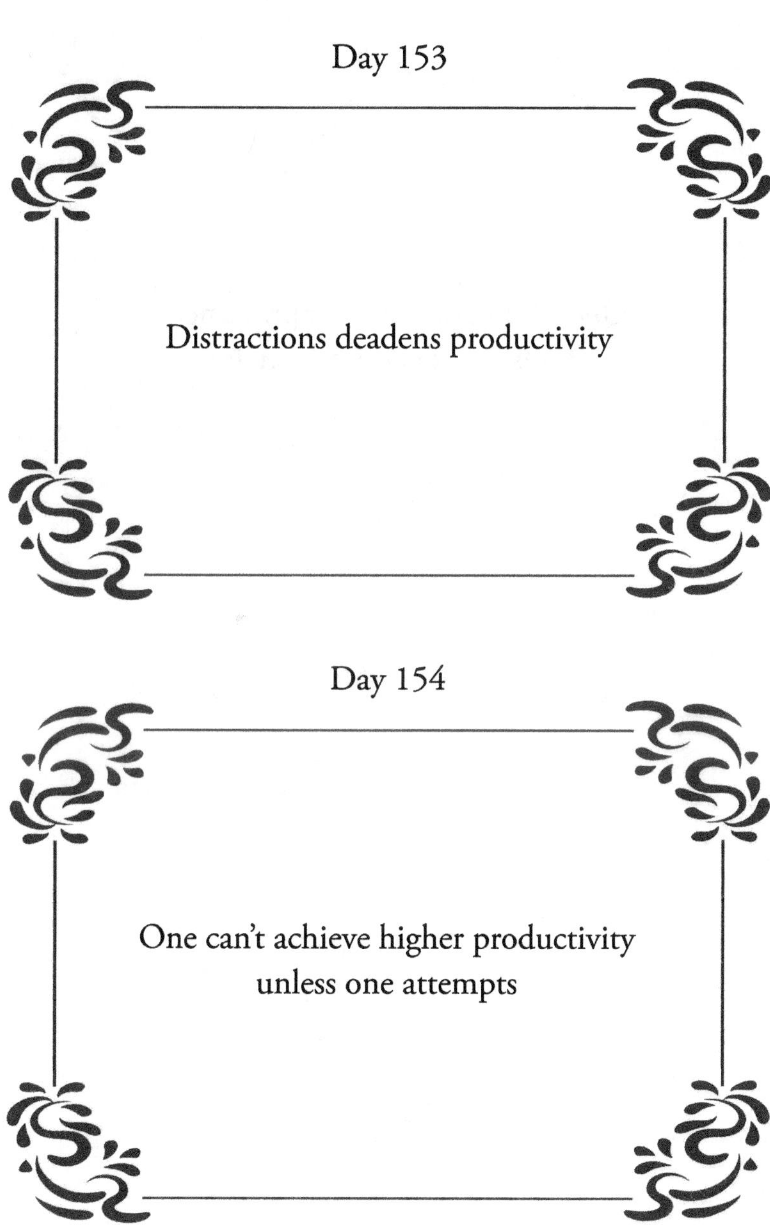

Distractions deadens productivity

Day 154

One can't achieve higher productivity
unless one attempts

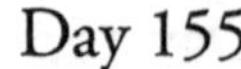

Day 155

Quest for continuous improvement
leads to higher productivity

Day 156

Be in the company of
productive people

Day 157

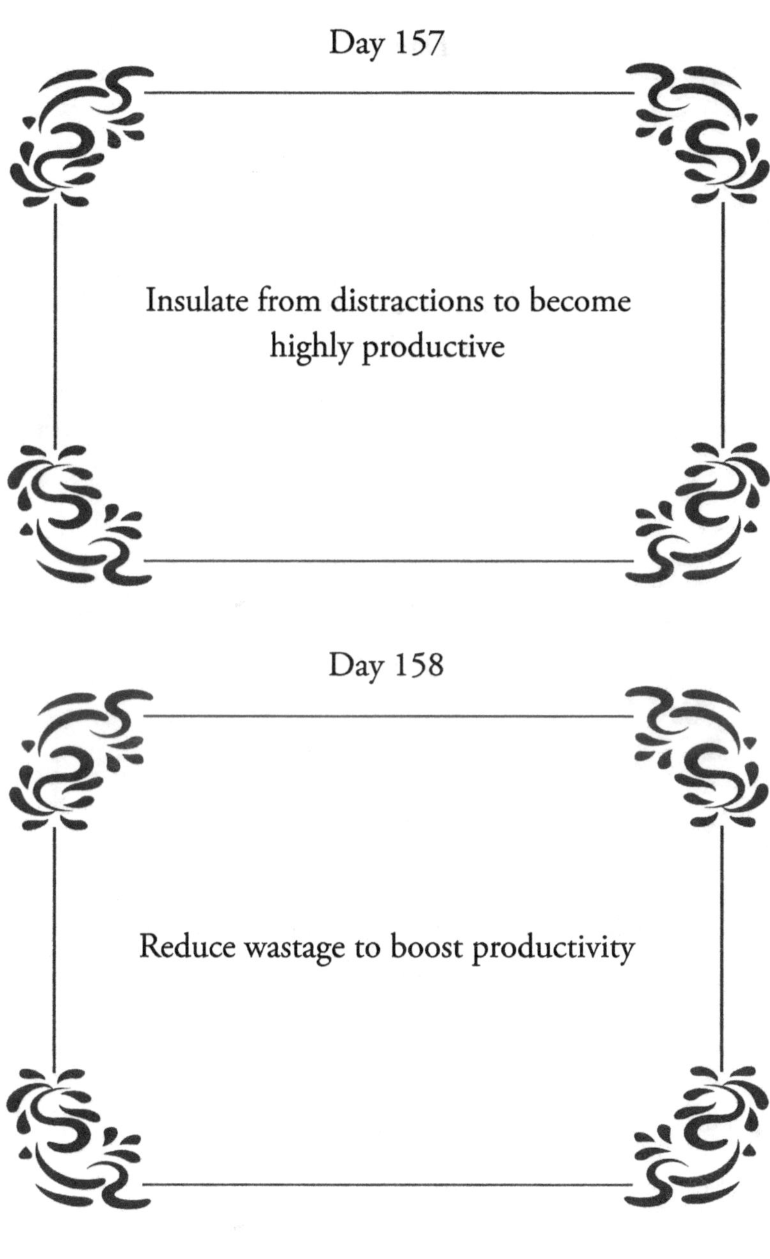

Insulate from distractions to become highly productive

Day 158

Reduce wastage to boost productivity

Day 159

Too much rest causes that much rust on productivity

Day 160

Right choices and right actions lead to increased productivity

Day 161

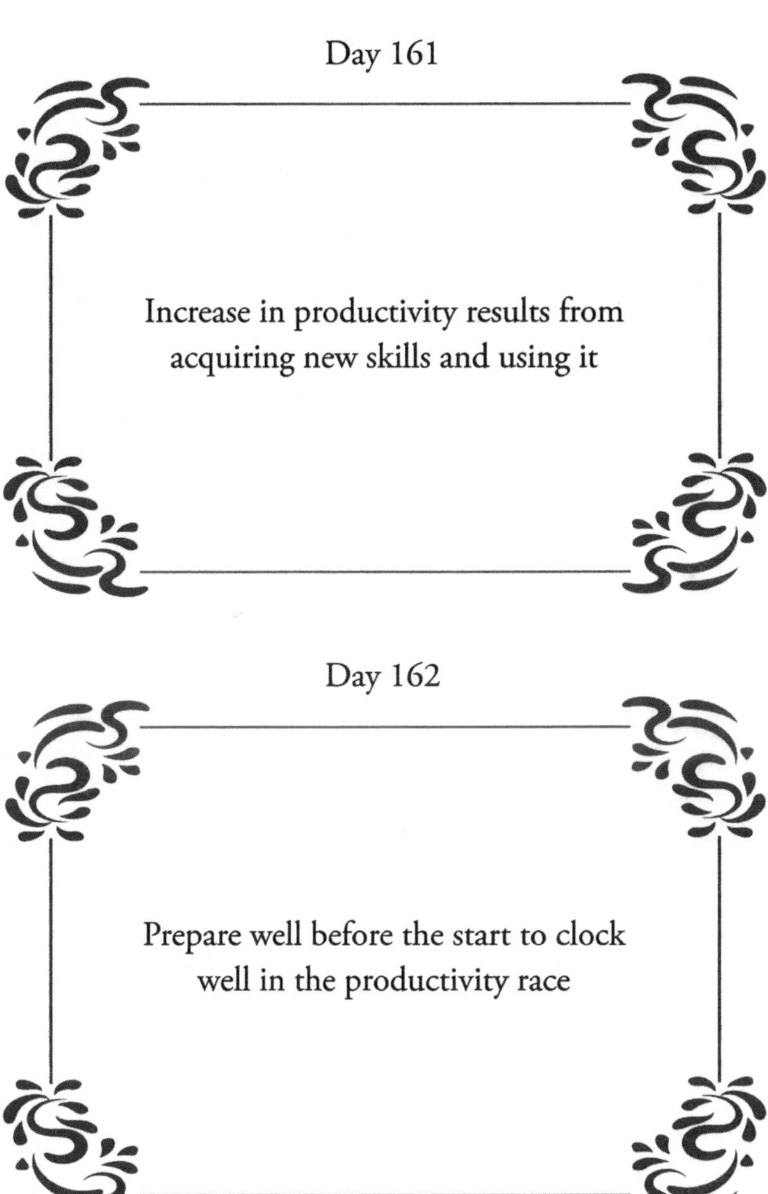

Increase in productivity results from acquiring new skills and using it

Day 162

Prepare well before the start to clock well in the productivity race

Day 163

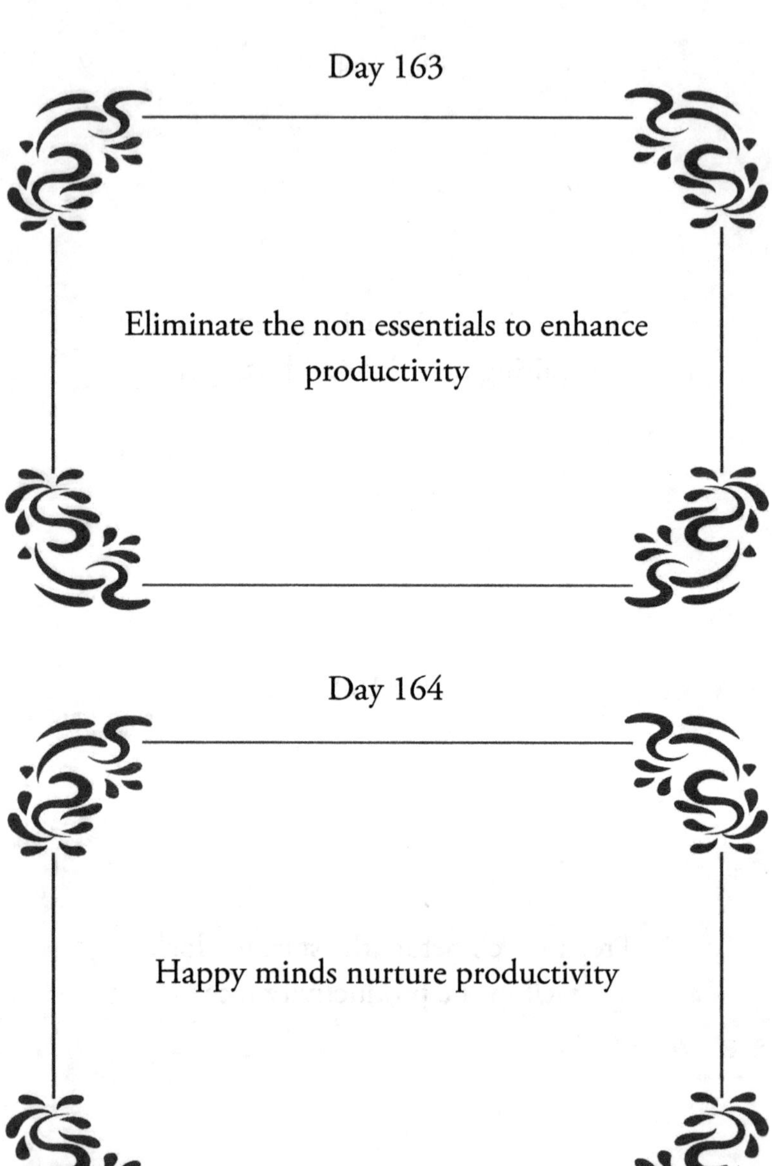

Eliminate the non essentials to enhance productivity

Day 164

Happy minds nurture productivity

Day 165

Be confident, You too can achieve higher productivity

Day 166

When one enjoys work, productivity soars

Day 167

Passion and reason drive productivity

Day 168

Prioritize to become productive

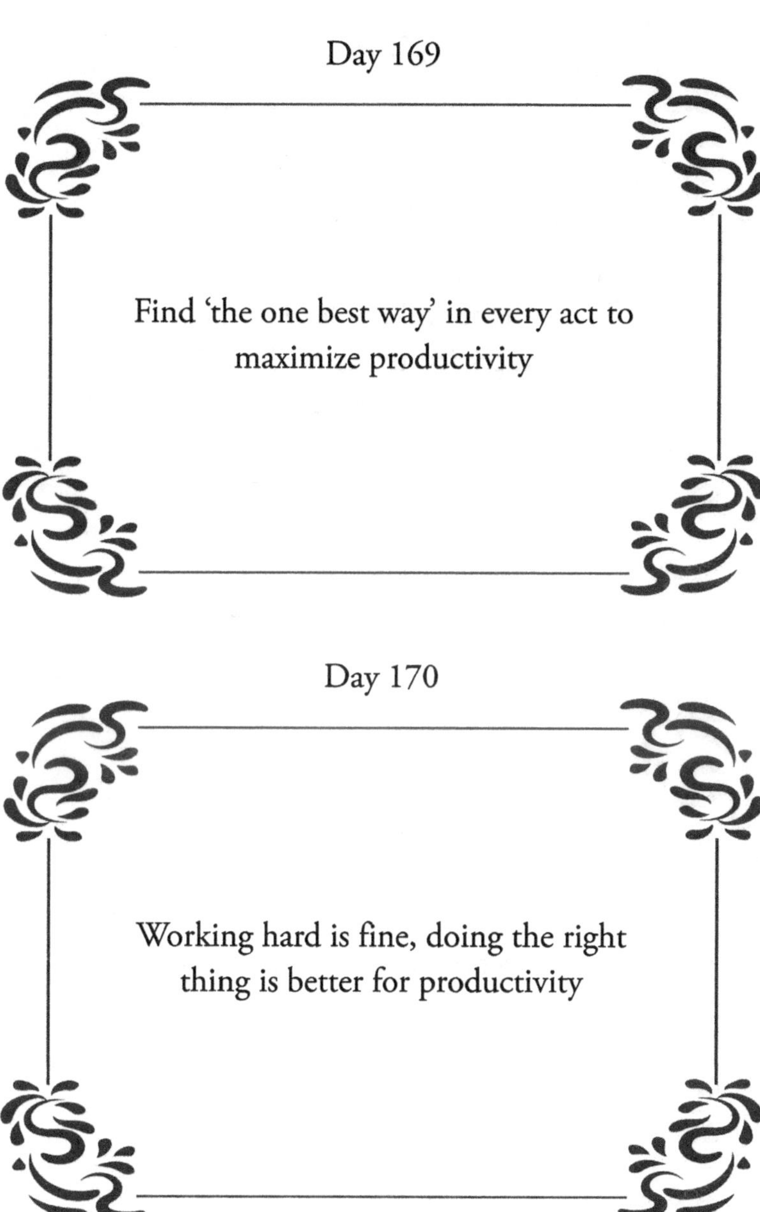

Day 169

Find 'the one best way' in every act to maximize productivity

Day 170

Working hard is fine, doing the right thing is better for productivity

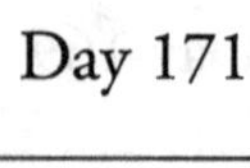
Day 171

Talent alone will not lead to higher productivity, the attitudes will

Day 172

Engage technologies to be productive

Day 173

Software solutions take the burden away to be productive

Day 174

Go for a continuous improvement plan to gain on productivity

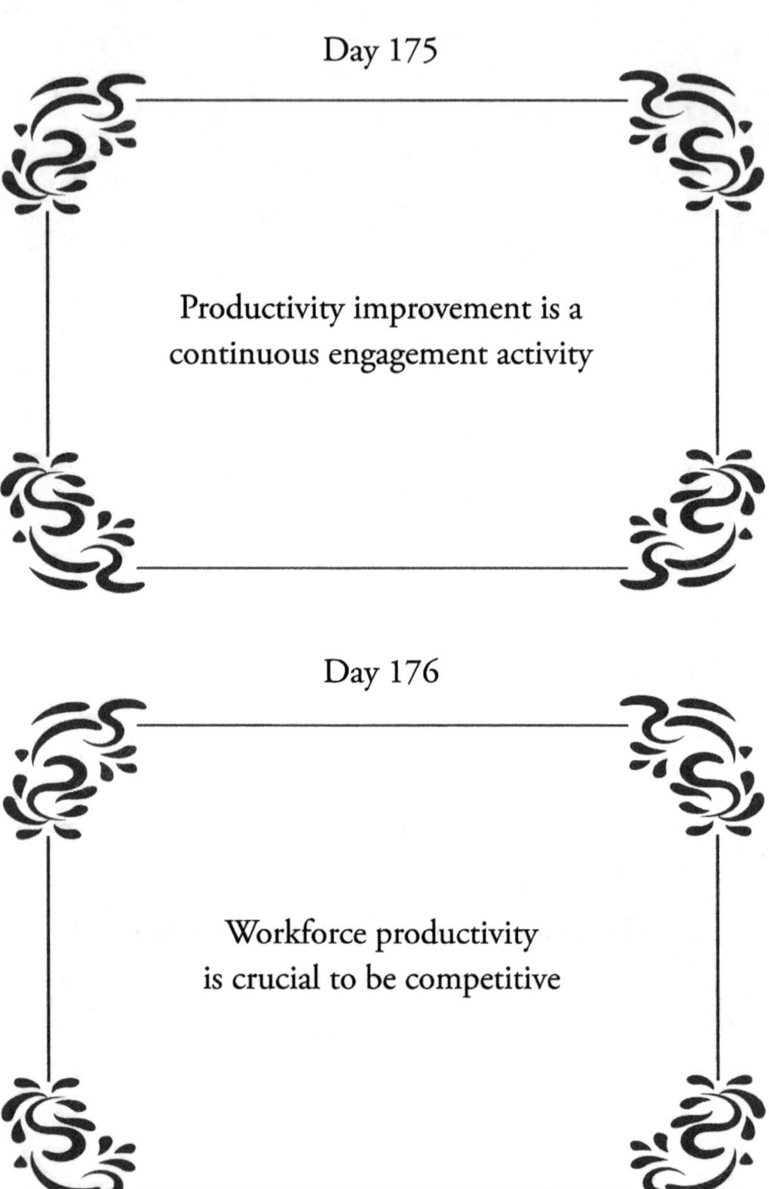

Day 175

Productivity improvement is a continuous engagement activity

Day 176

Workforce productivity is crucial to be competitive

Day 177

Flexible working improves productivity

Day 178

Happy employees are better engaged to be productive

Day 179

Appreciation fuels productivity

Day 180

Updating knowledge and skills makes one productive

Day 181

Averting minor mistakes can make a big difference in productivity

Day 182

Collaboration is the key driver of productivity

Day 183

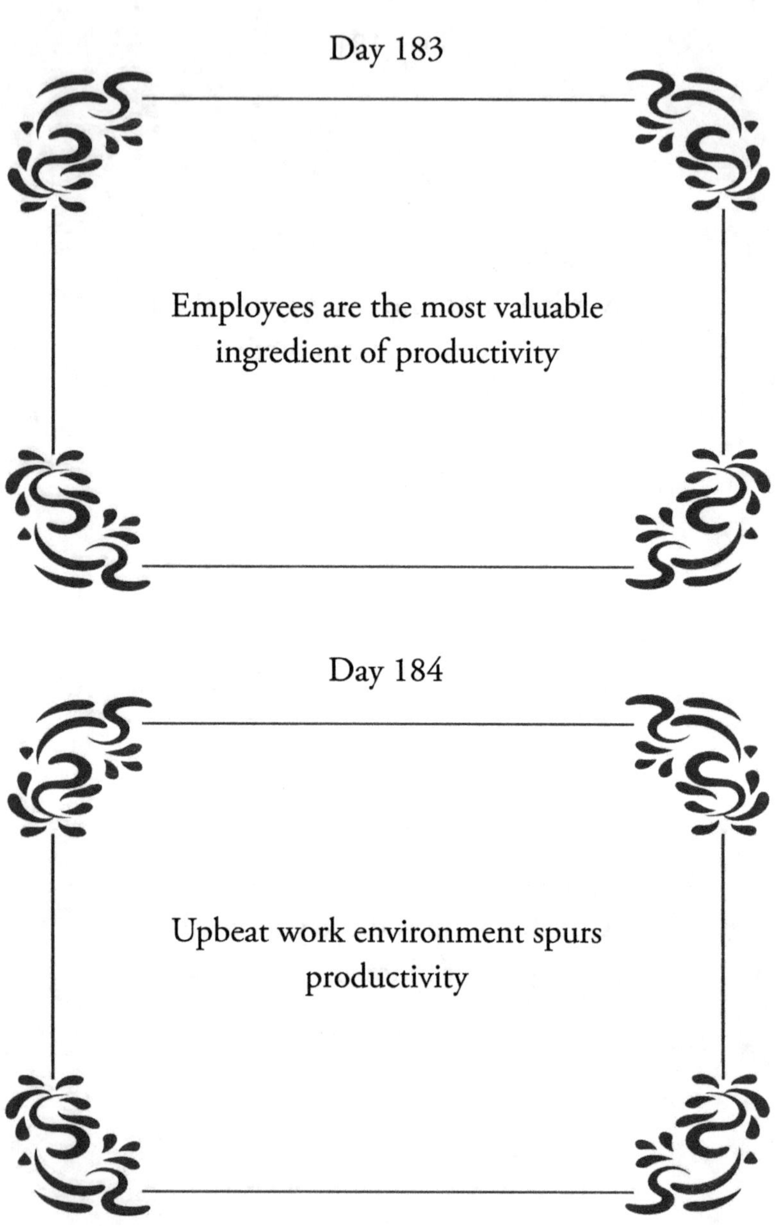

Employees are the most valuable ingredient of productivity

Day 184

Upbeat work environment spurs productivity

Day 185

Engrossing in social media while at work is counterproductive

Day 186

Turning off the personal phone while at work increases productivity

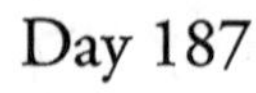

Day 187

Right technology and methods ensure increased productivity

Day 188

Automate processes and workflows for higher productivity

Day 189

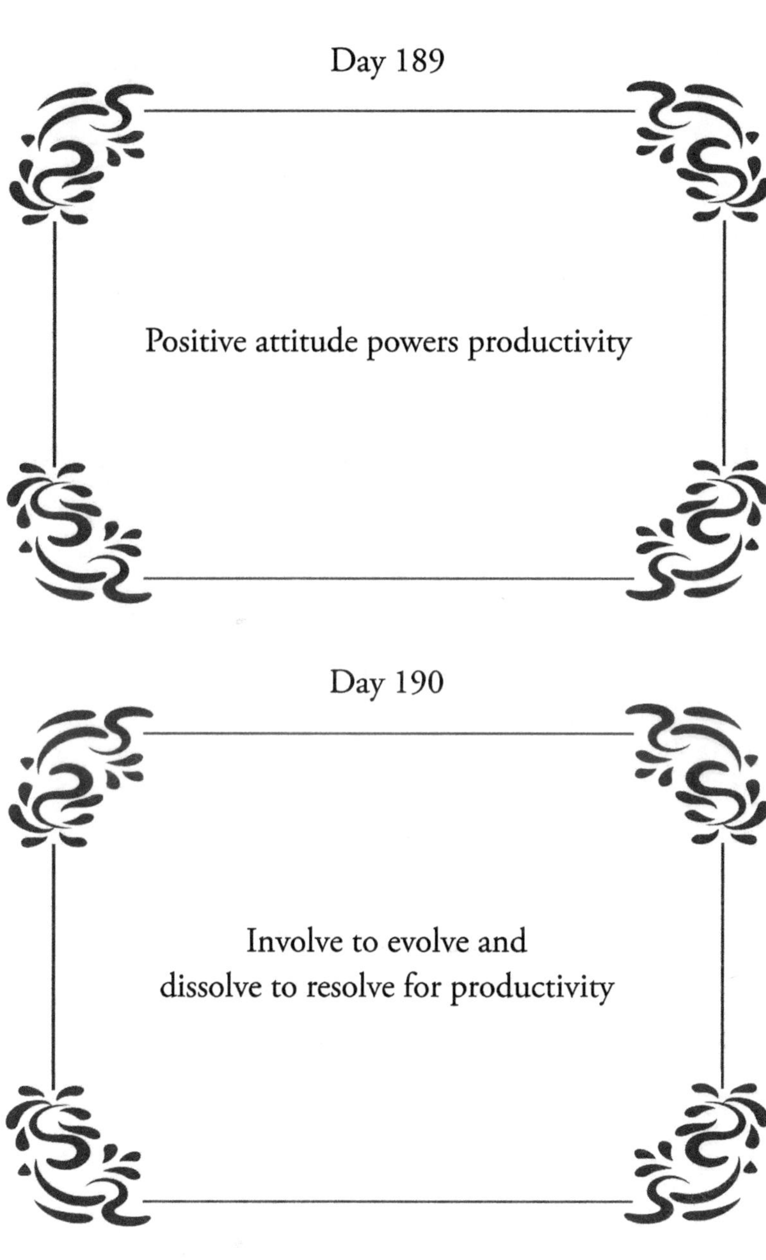

Positive attitude powers productivity

Day 190

Involve to evolve and
dissolve to resolve for productivity

Day 191

Be proactive to become productive

Day 192

Productivity decides
the wealth of a nation

Day 193

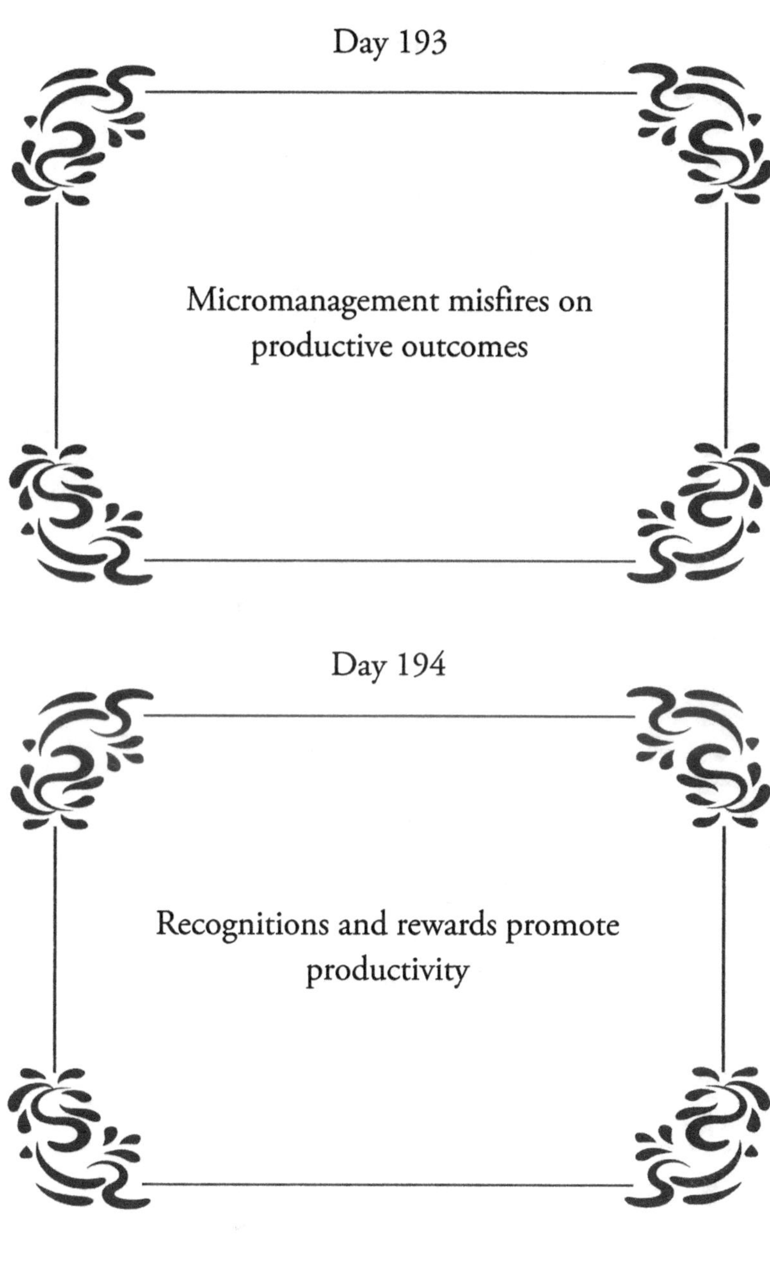

Micromanagement misfires on productive outcomes

Day 194

Recognitions and rewards promote productivity

Day 195

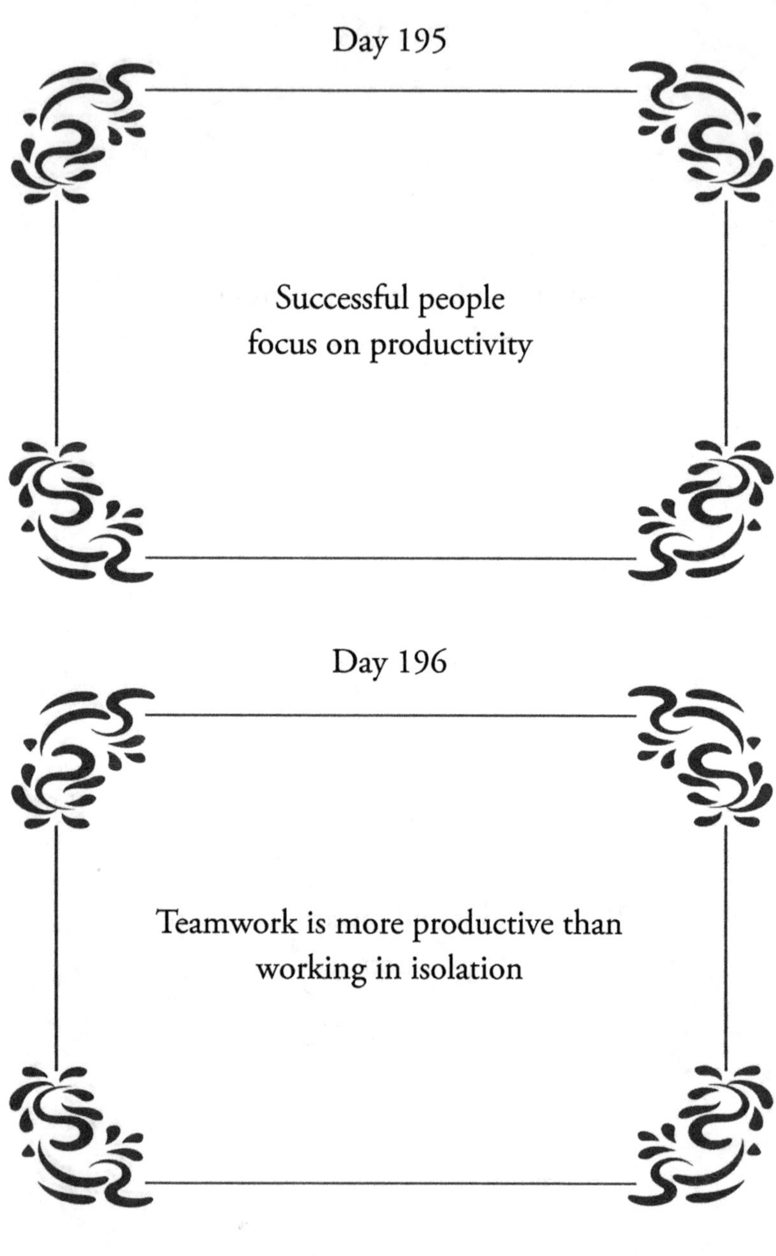

Successful people
focus on productivity

Day 196

Teamwork is more productive than
working in isolation

Day 197

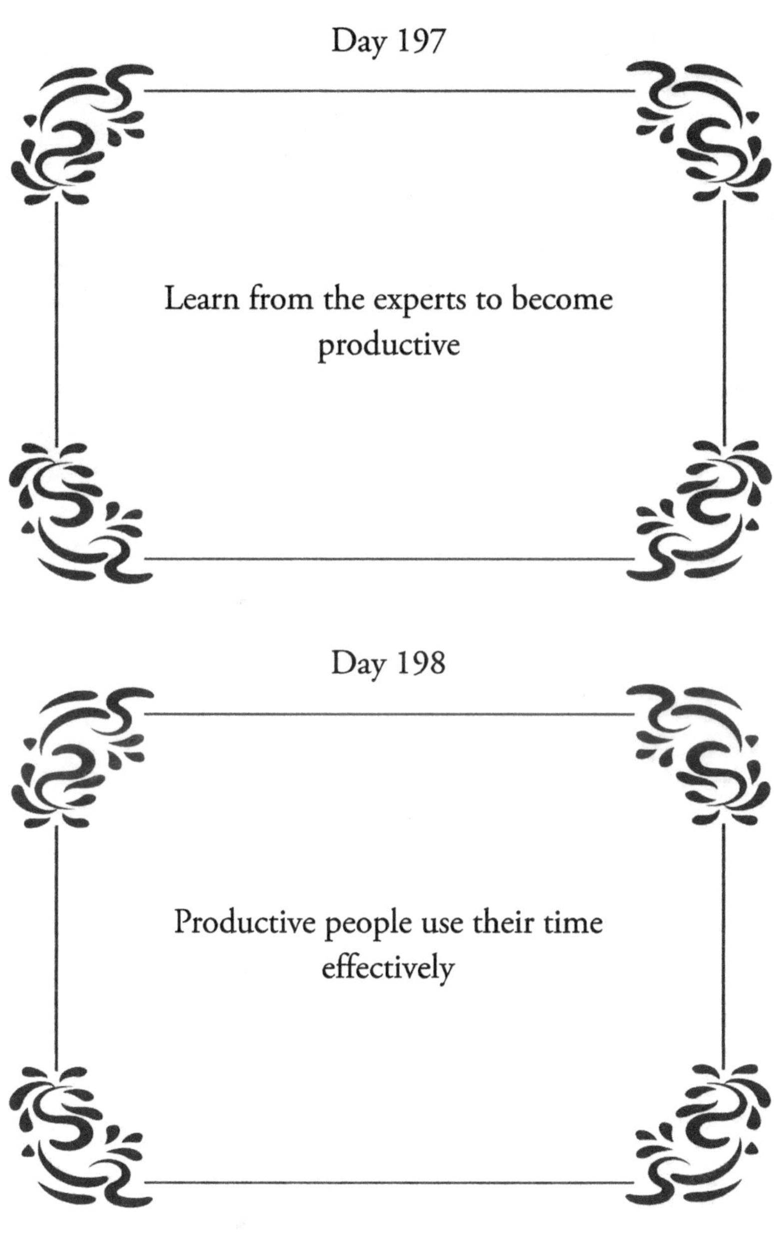

Learn from the experts to become productive

Day 198

Productive people use their time effectively

Day 199

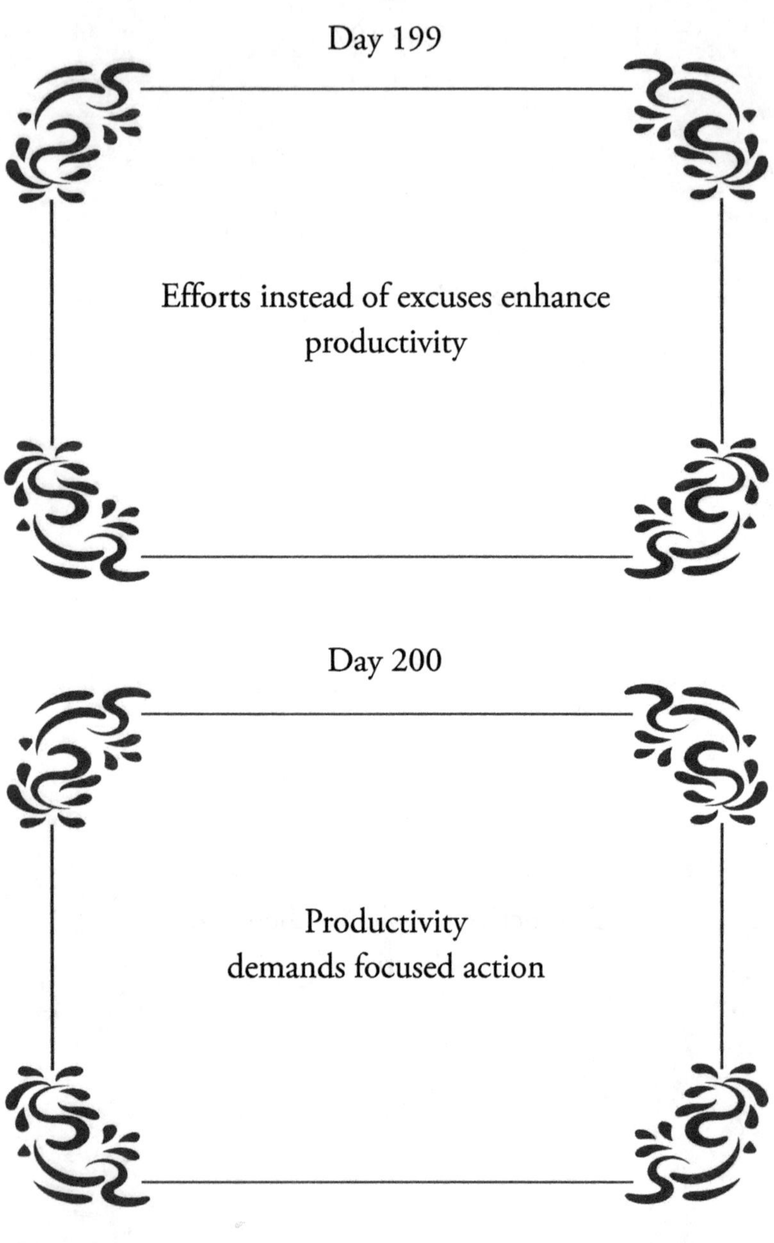

Efforts instead of excuses enhance productivity

Day 200

Productivity demands focused action

Day 201

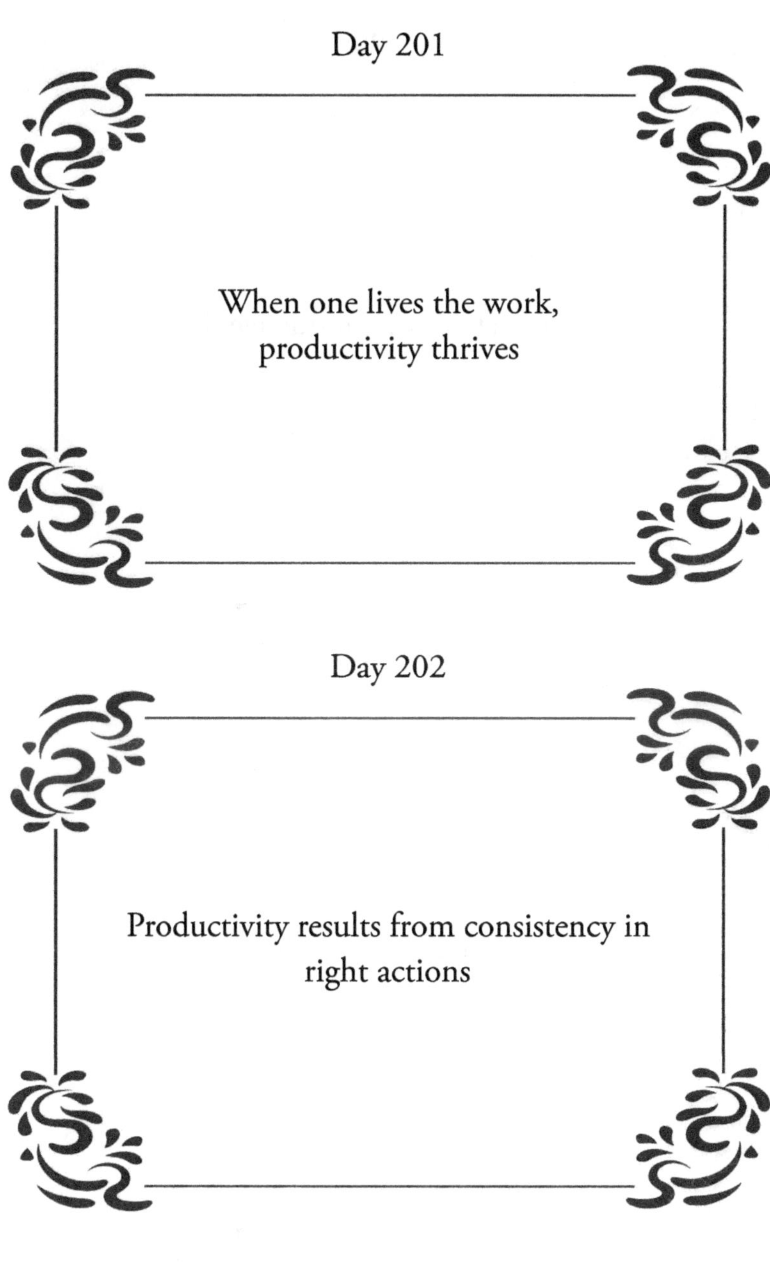

When one lives the work,
productivity thrives

Day 202

Productivity results from consistency in right actions

Day 203

Make every day a productive day

Day 204

Be positive to be productive

Day 205

When one starts enjoying one's work, the productivity blooms

Day 206

Be relevant, realistic and reasonable to become productive

Day 207

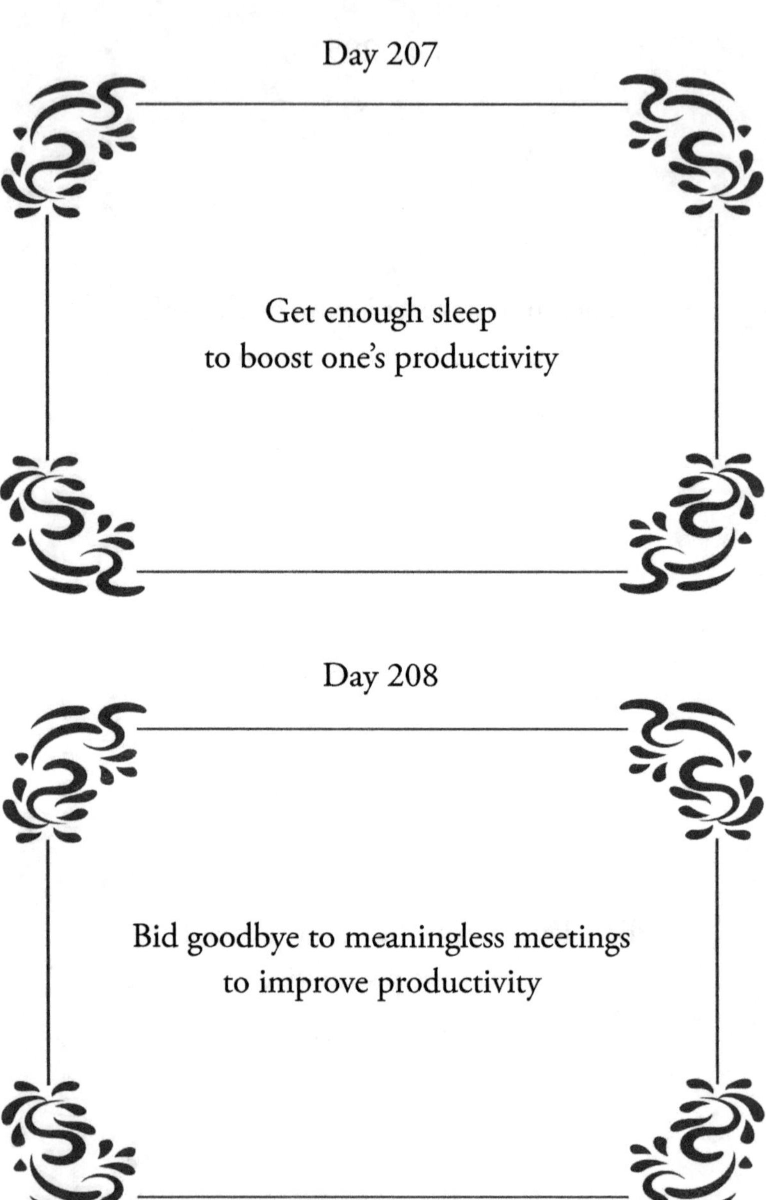

Get enough sleep
to boost one's productivity

Day 208

Bid goodbye to meaningless meetings
to improve productivity

Day 209

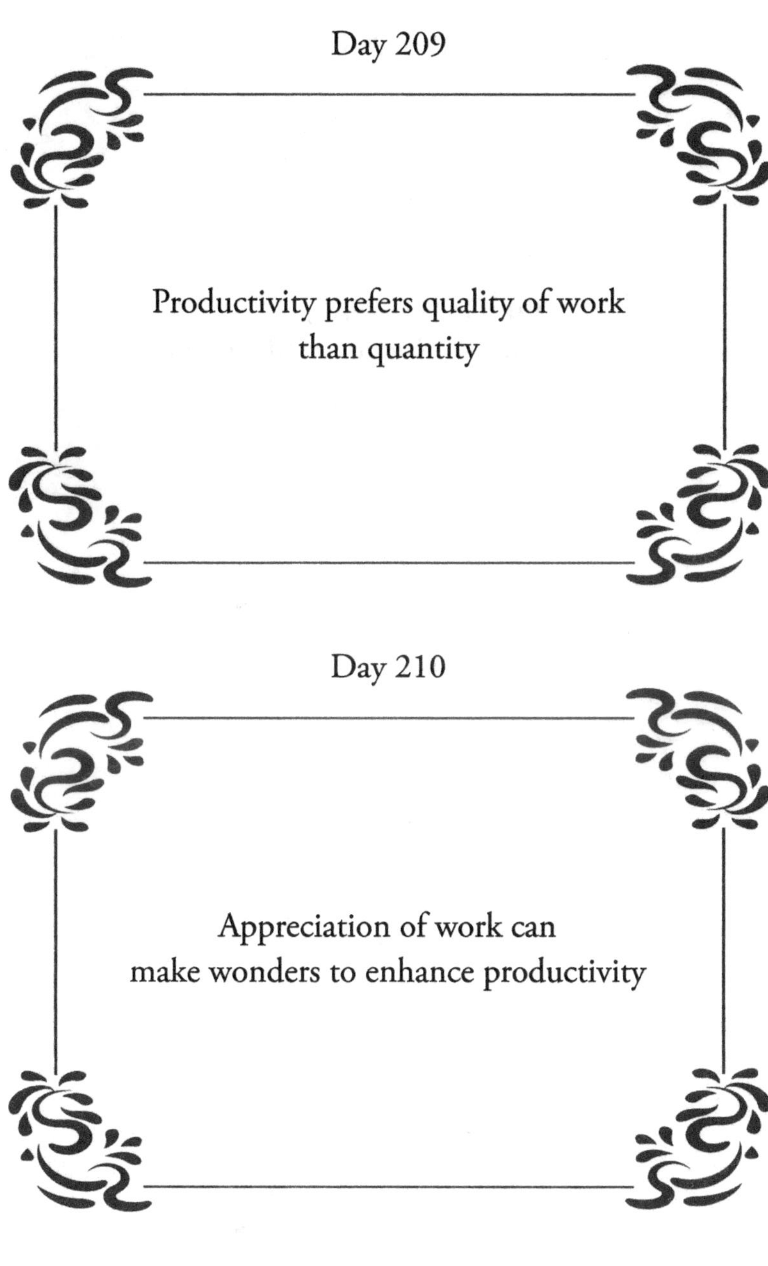

Productivity prefers quality of work than quantity

Day 210

Appreciation of work can make wonders to enhance productivity

Day 211

Keep employees engaged, motivated and happy for higher productivity

Day 212

An engaged employee is more productive than the disengaged

Day 213

The feel of getting recognized makes one more productive

Day 214

Patience in listening to the complaints help improve productivity

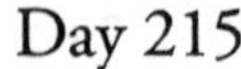

Day 215

Taking care of employees boosts productivity

Day 216

Differentiating urgent to important, is important in improving productivity

Day 217

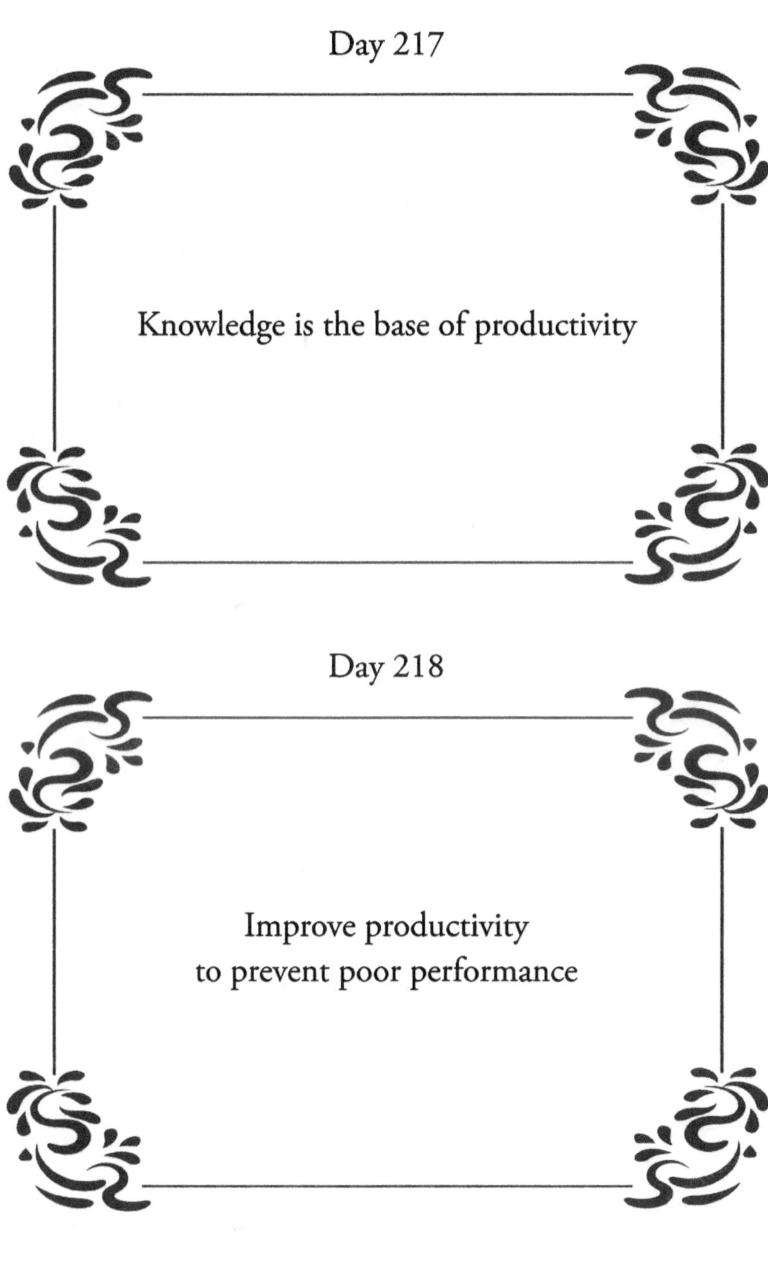

Knowledge is the base of productivity

Day 218

Improve productivity
to prevent poor performance

Day 219

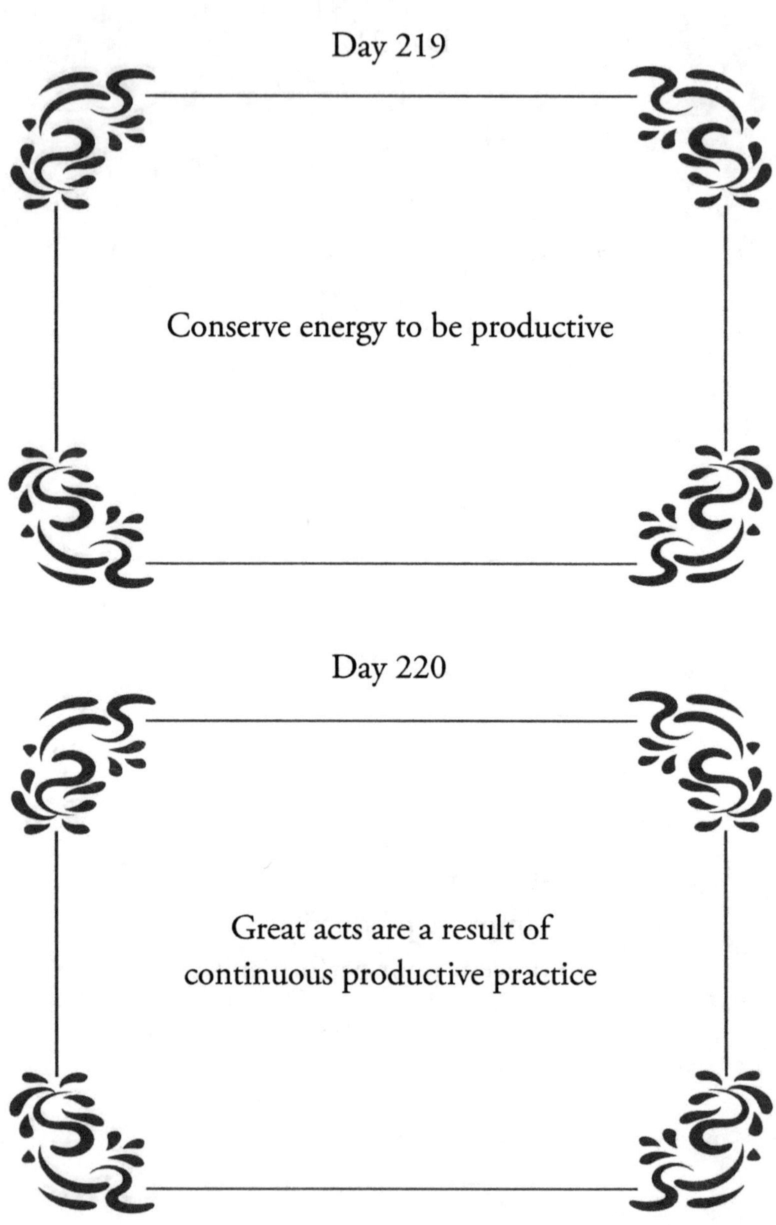

Conserve energy to be productive

Day 220

Great acts are a result of
continuous productive practice

Day 221

Adapt good practices to enhance productivity

Day 222

Leaning on the disempowered team is a loss on productivity

Day 223

Be the ambassador of
productive actions

Day 224

Be at your best when it concerns
productivity

Day 225

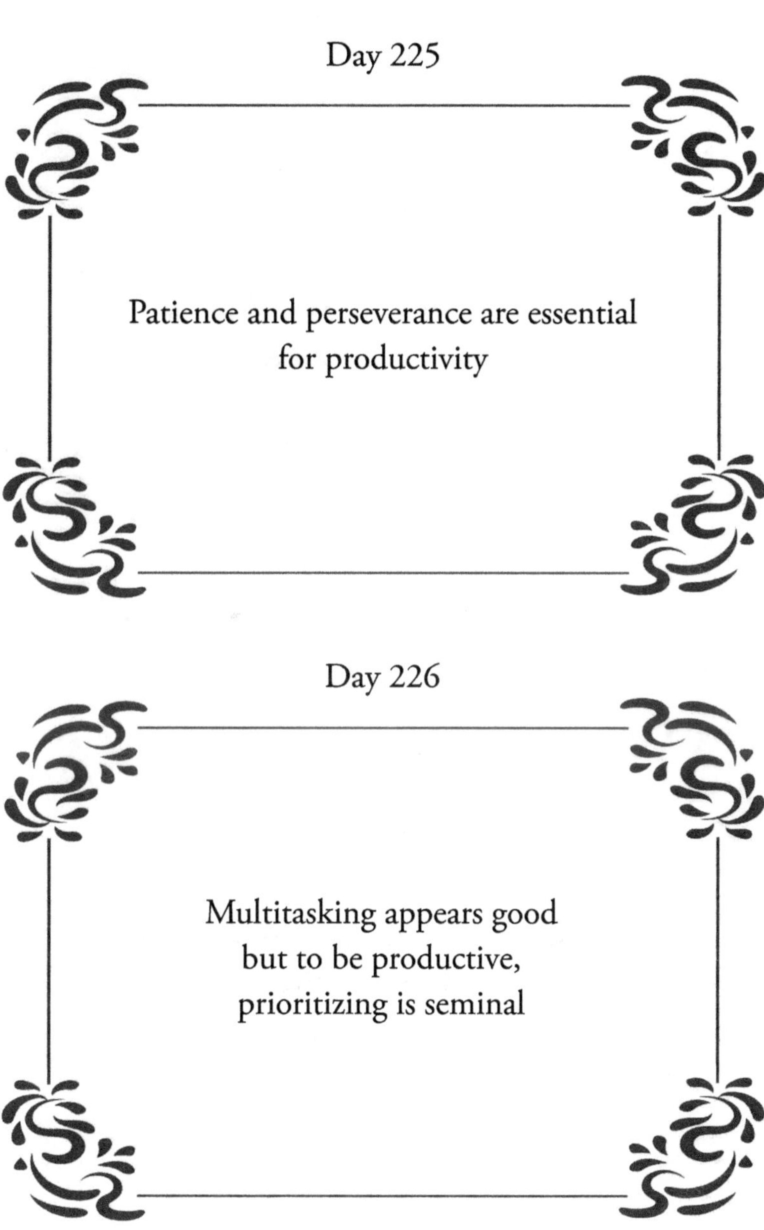

Patience and perseverance are essential for productivity

Day 226

Multitasking appears good but to be productive, prioritizing is seminal

Day 227

Productivity rests on leadership that creates opportunities

Day 228

Cry not over failure, take the learnings to be productive

Day 229

Opportunities to be productive are all around, find it and act on it

Day 230

Never imagine you can't achieve higher productivity

Day 231

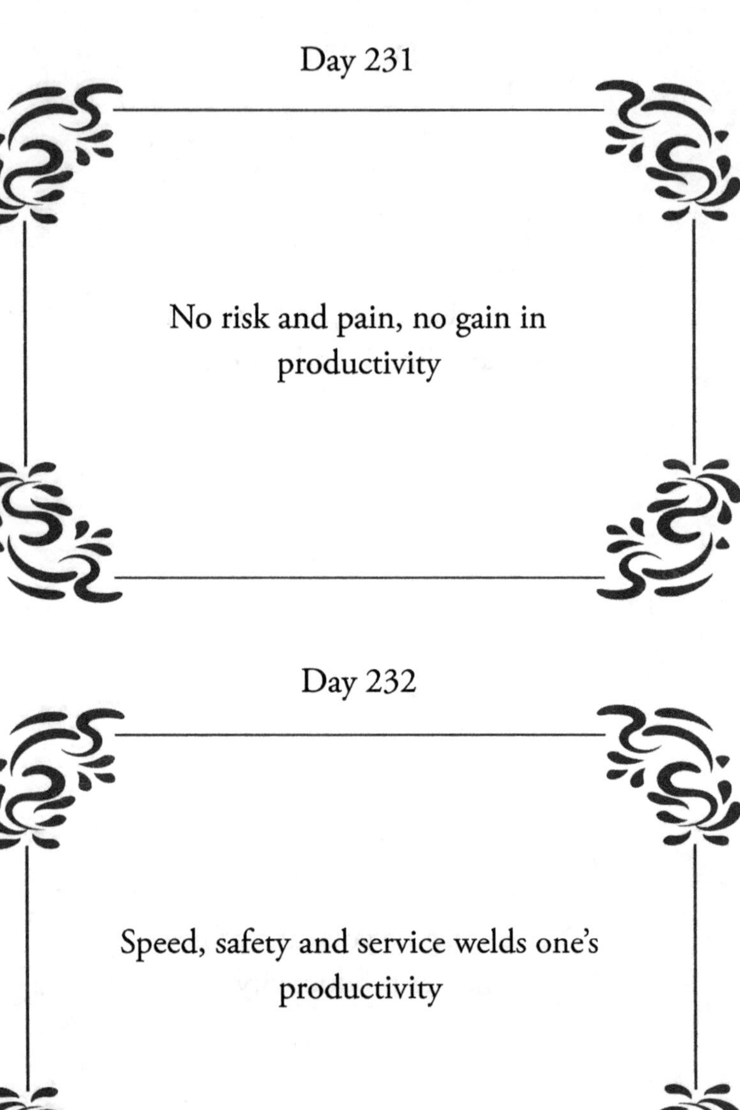

No risk and pain, no gain in productivity

Day 232

Speed, safety and service welds one's productivity

Day 233

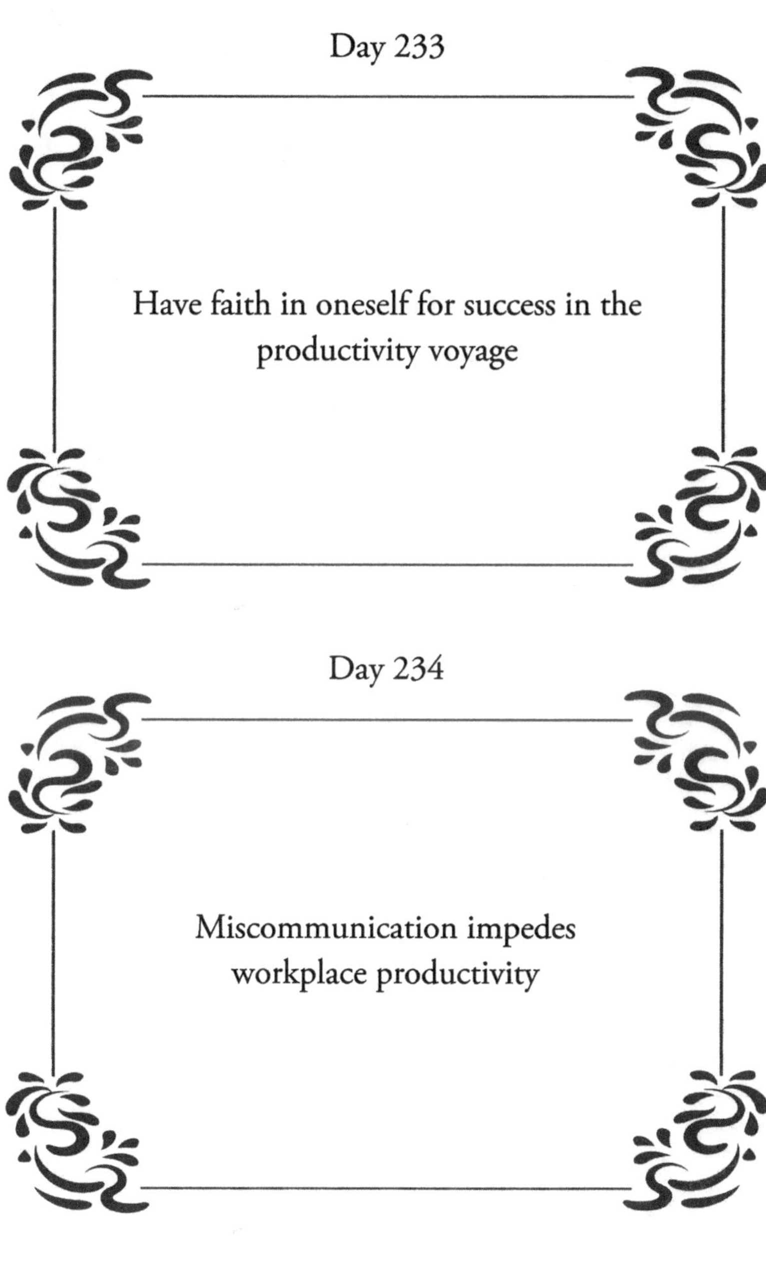

Have faith in oneself for success in the productivity voyage

Day 234

Miscommunication impedes workplace productivity

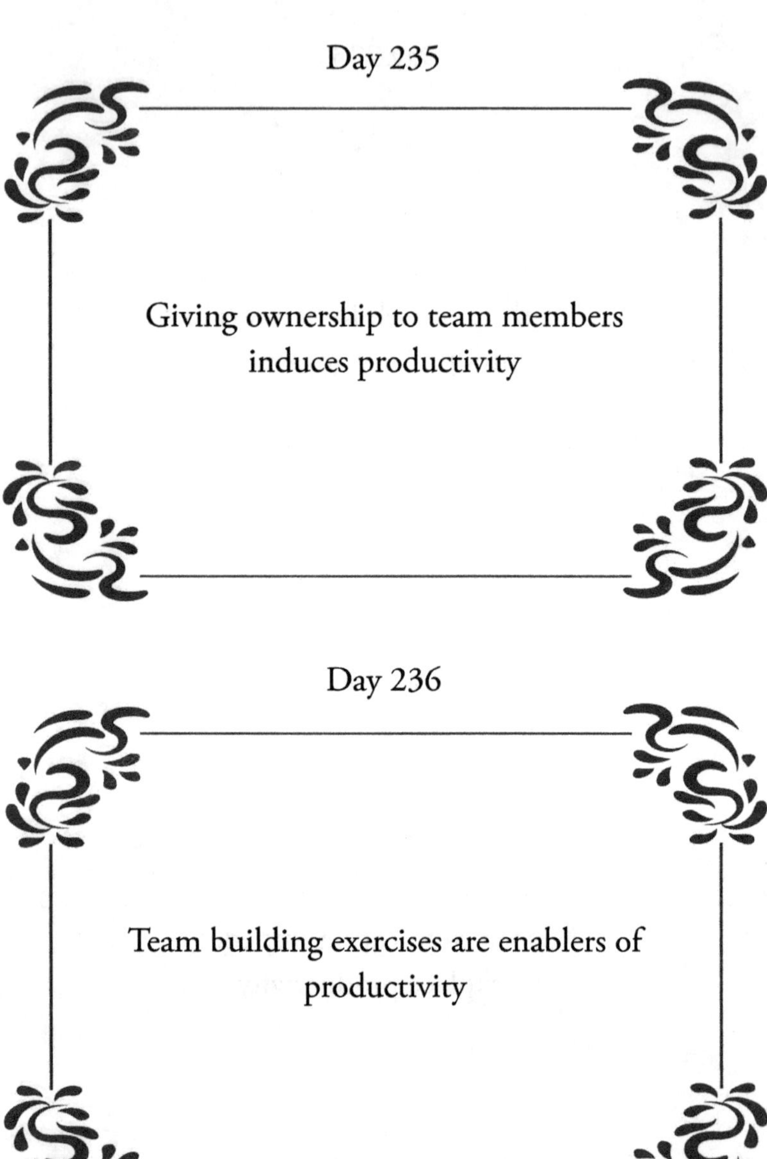

Day 235

Giving ownership to team members induces productivity

Day 236

Team building exercises are enablers of productivity

Day 237

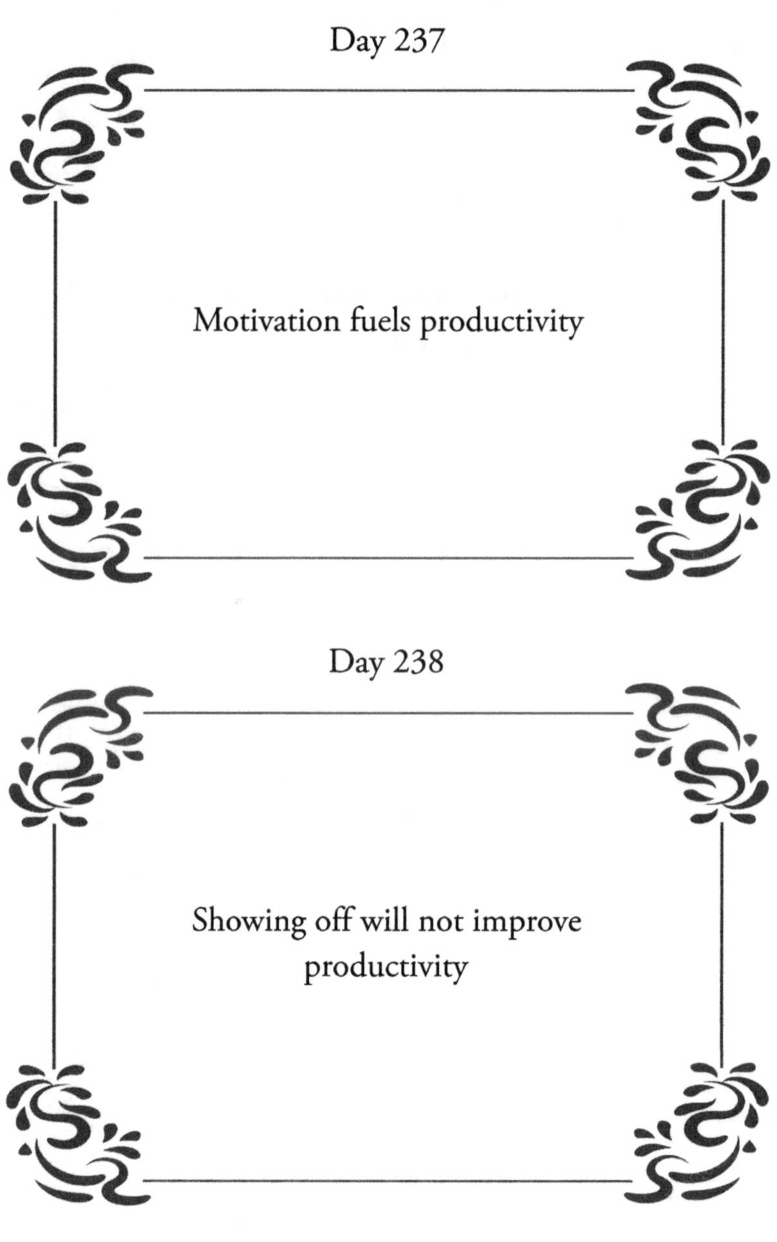

Motivation fuels productivity

Day 238

Showing off will not improve productivity

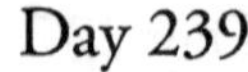

Day 239

Tomorrow implies indefiniteness in productivity

Day 240

Search for something new everyday to be productive

Day 241

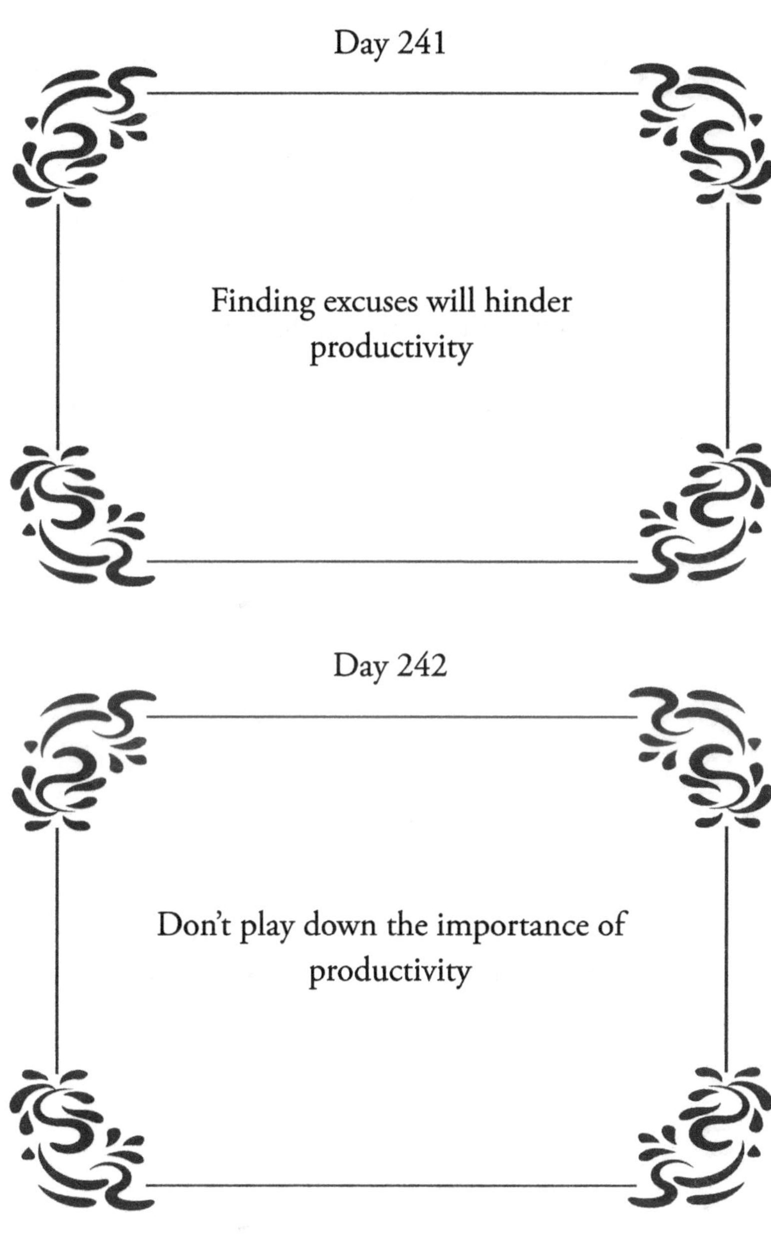

Finding excuses will hinder productivity

Day 242

Don't play down the importance of productivity

Day 243

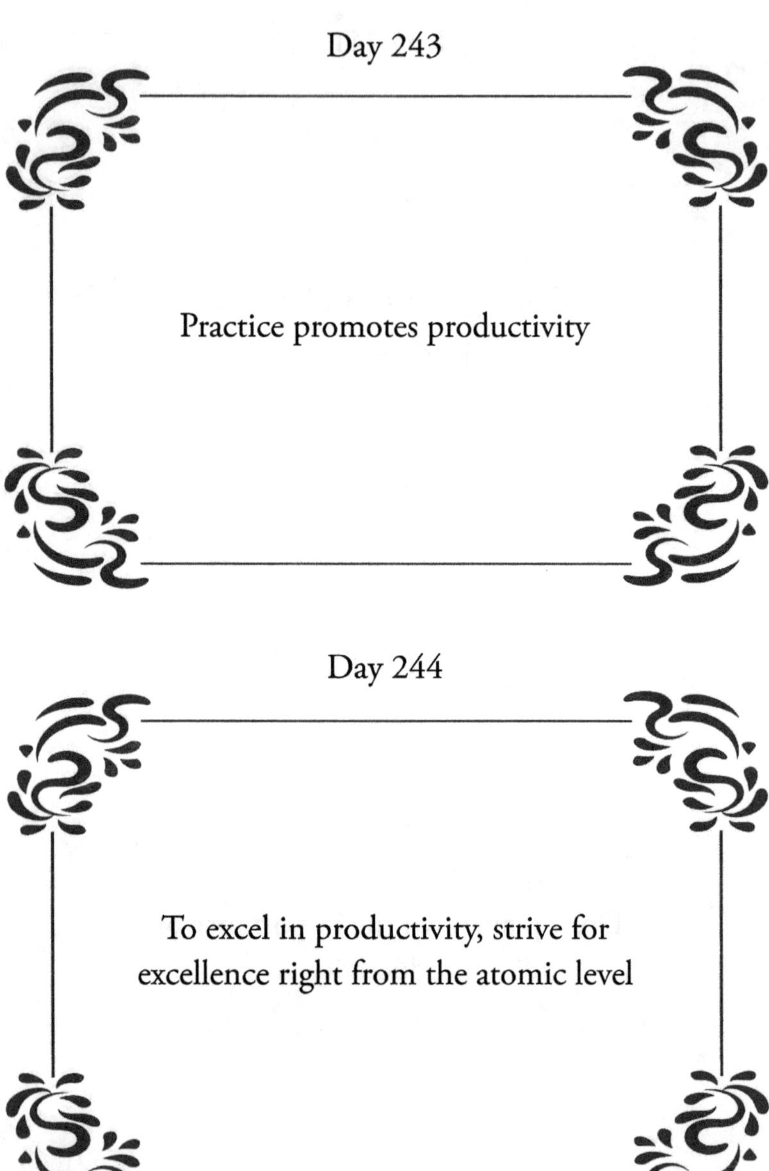

Practice promotes productivity

Day 244

To excel in productivity, strive for excellence right from the atomic level

Day 245

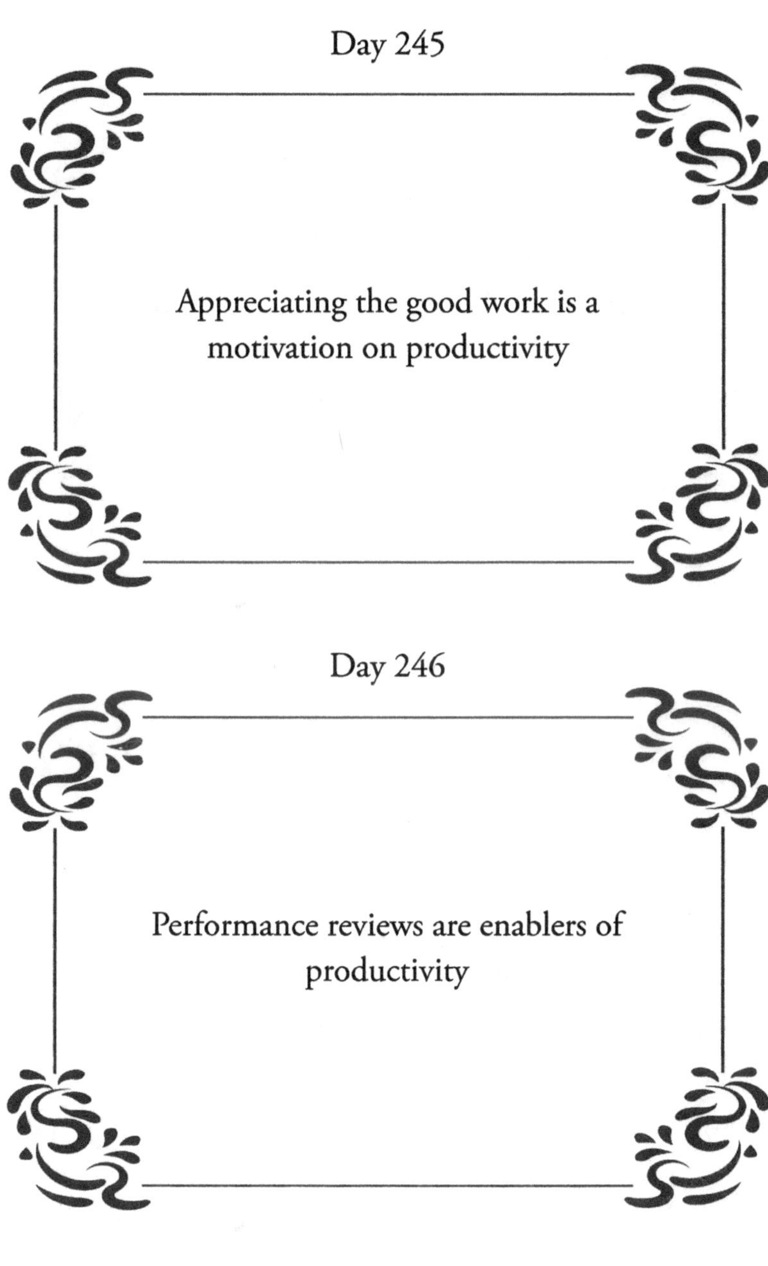

Appreciating the good work is a motivation on productivity

Day 246

Performance reviews are enablers of productivity

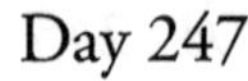

Day 247

Get rid of the organizational cobwebs
to increase productivity

Day 248

Focused engagement of mind ensues
higher productivity

Day 249

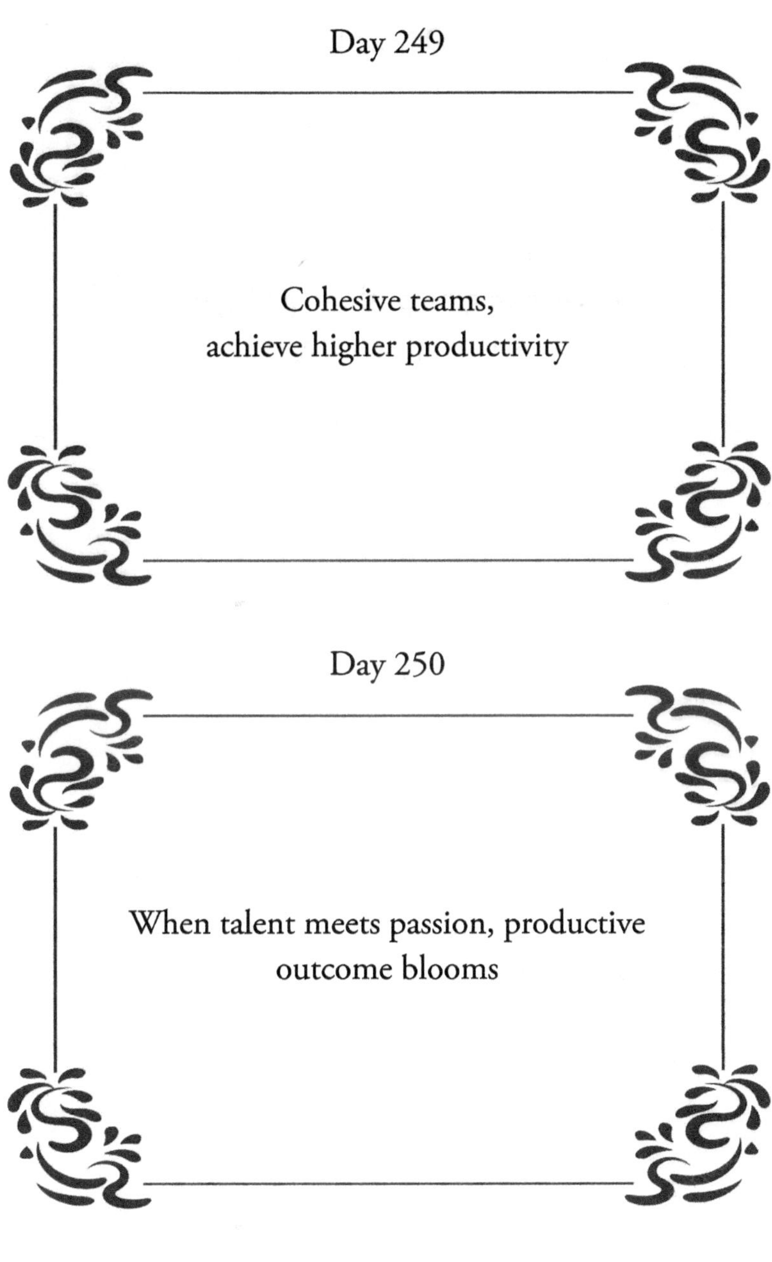

Cohesive teams,
achieve higher productivity

Day 250

When talent meets passion, productive
outcome blooms

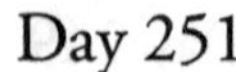

Day 251

An encouraging push, to go beyond, fetches productivity

Day 252

Setting inspiring vision for production teams is an organisational responsibility

Day 253

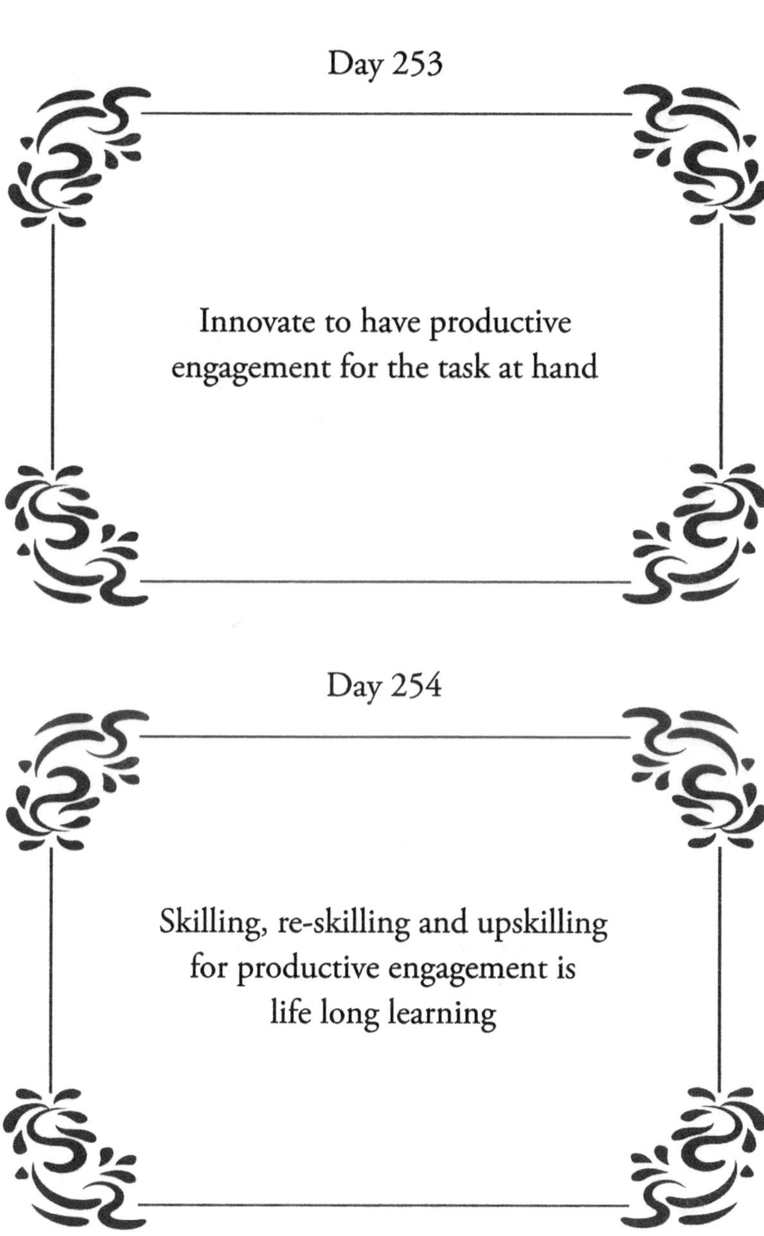

Innovate to have productive engagement for the task at hand

Day 254

Skilling, re-skilling and upskilling for productive engagement is life long learning

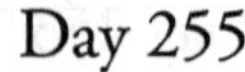

Day 255

The journey of productivity begins with learning and training

Day 256

The productive engagement evolves with learning to apply what is learned

Day 257

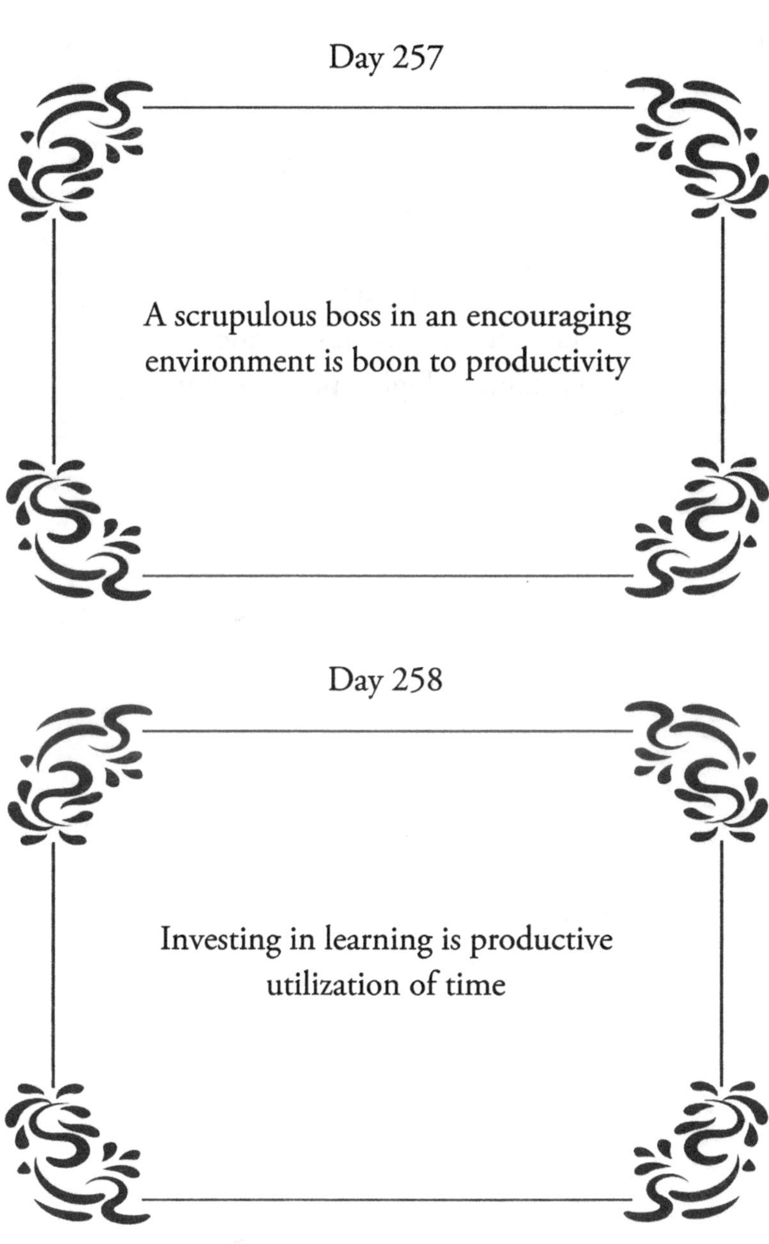

A scrupulous boss in an encouraging environment is boon to productivity

Day 258

Investing in learning is productive utilization of time

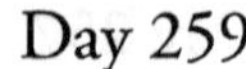

Day 259

Nothing can beat
persistence and perseverance
in achieving higher productivity

Day 260

Capture the composite factors of
productivity for
productive engagement

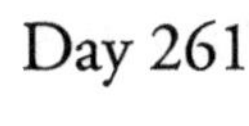

Day 261

An orderly workplace encourages productivity

Day 262

Talent, motivation and attitude decide the achievement in productivity

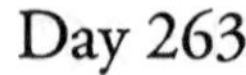

Day 263

Be like the sword that snicks
unproductive sprouts

Day 264

Success in productivity awaits those
who take the plunge

Day 265

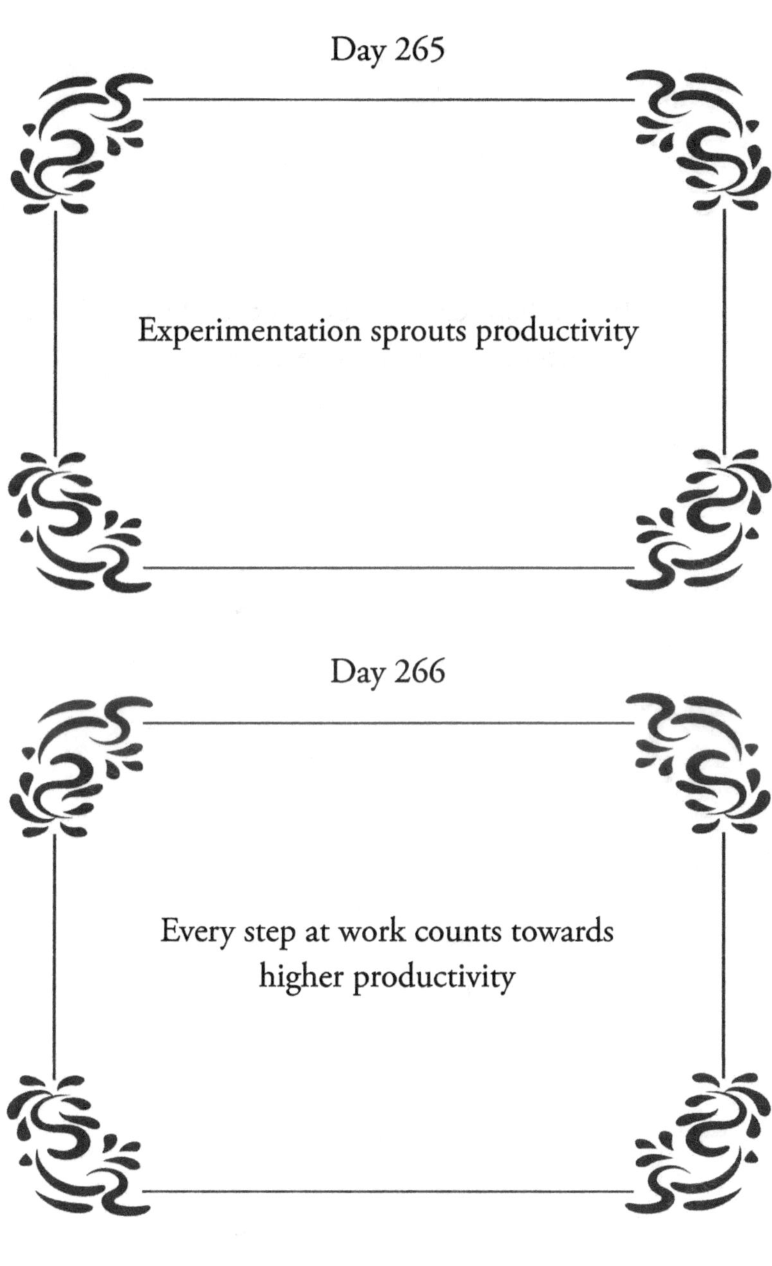

Experimentation sprouts productivity

Day 266

Every step at work counts towards higher productivity

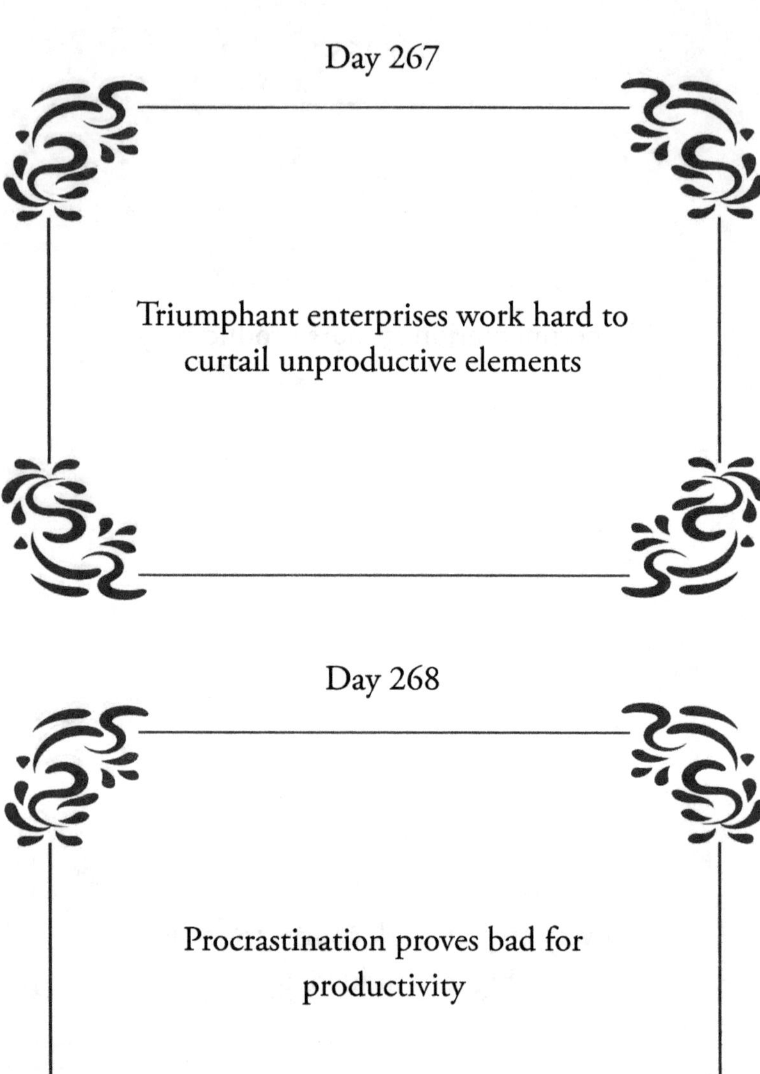

Day 267

Triumphant enterprises work hard to curtail unproductive elements

Day 268

Procrastination proves bad for productivity

Day 269

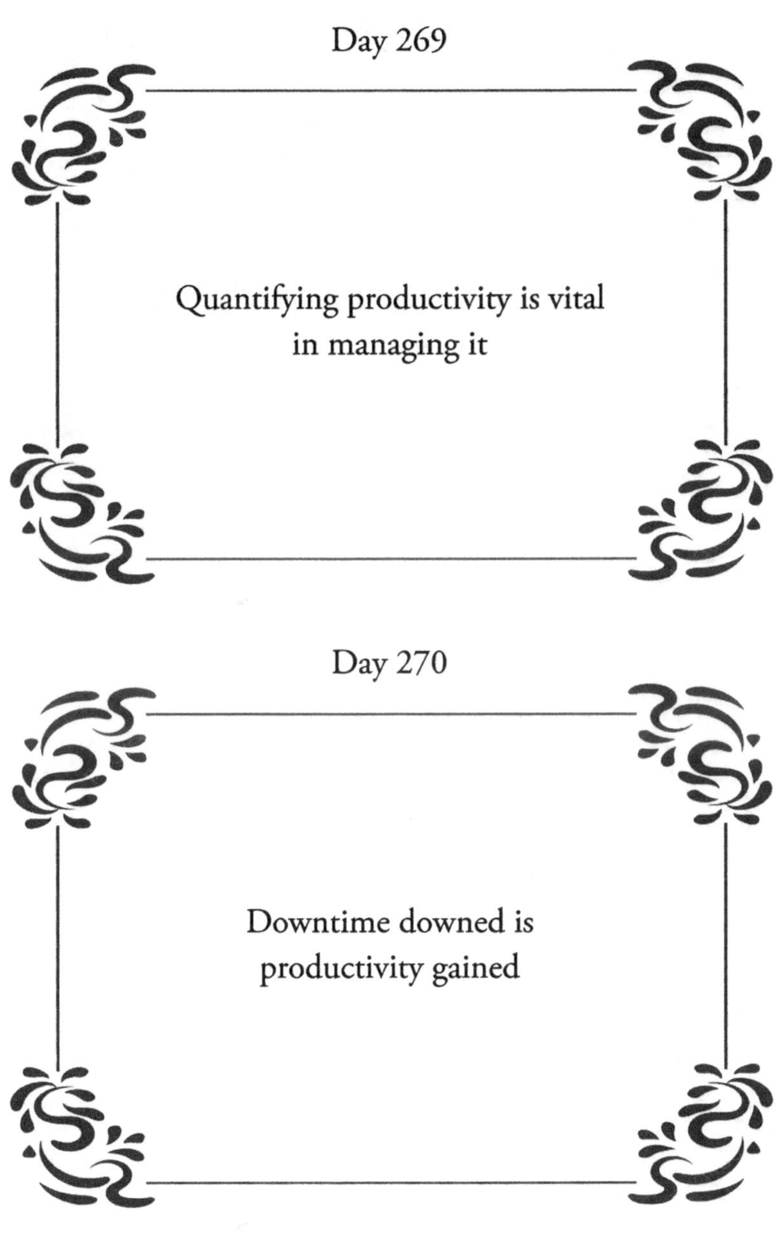

Quantifying productivity is vital in managing it

Day 270

Downtime downed is productivity gained

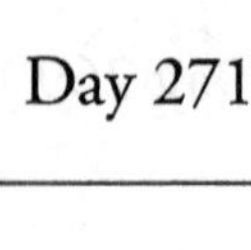

Day 271

Results speak louder than the claims in productivity

Day 272

Documentation matters a lot for achieving higher productivity

Day 273

Security and comfort foster productivity

Day 274

Studied, rational and prudent actions spur productivity

Day 275

Fear not the failure, it's a good teacher in productivity

Day 276

Time spent on sharpening the tools is an investment in productivity

Day 277

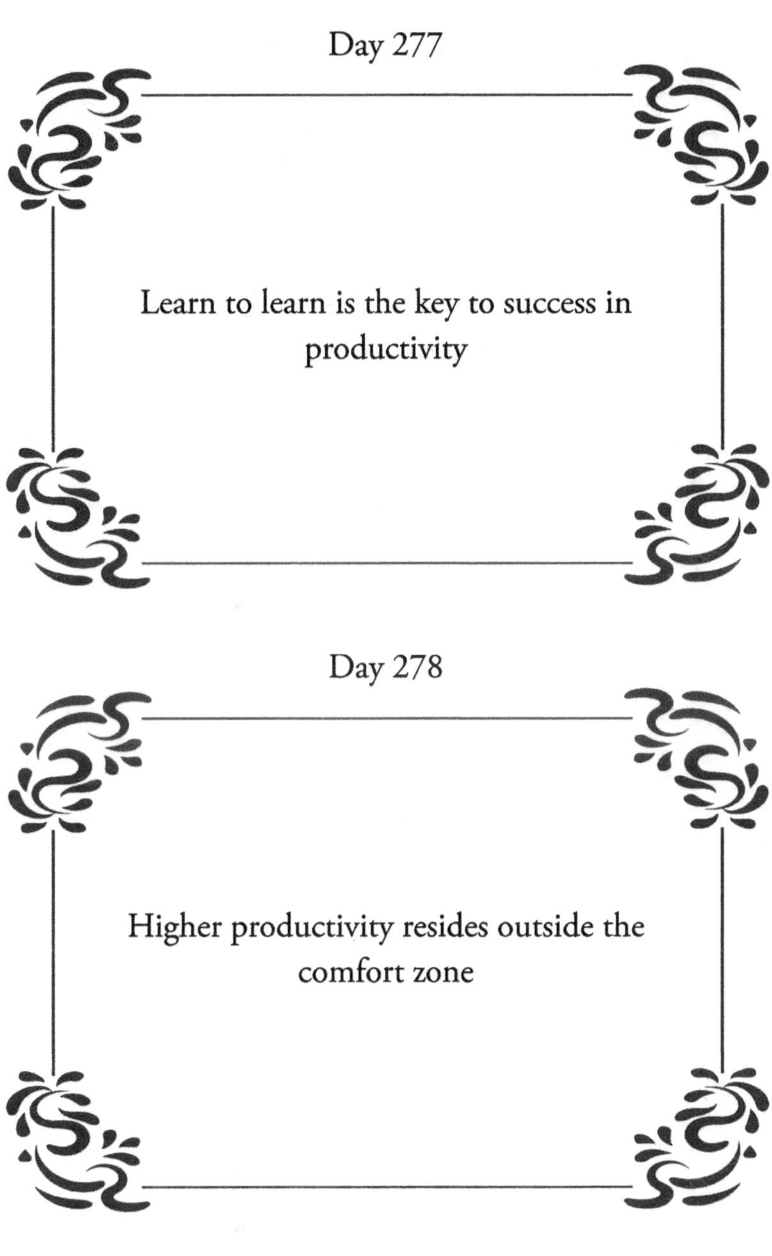

Learn to learn is the key to success in productivity

Day 278

Higher productivity resides outside the comfort zone

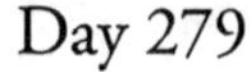

Day 279

Foresight is a virtue essential for success in productivity

Day 280

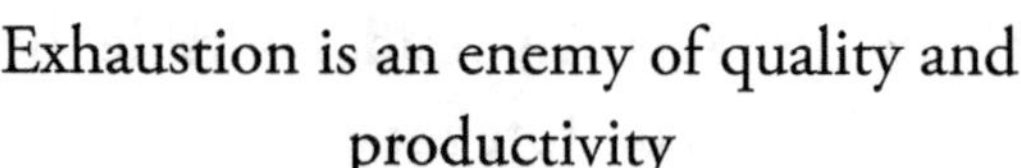

Exhaustion is an enemy of quality and productivity

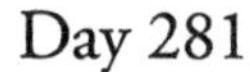

Day 281

Identify the essential and eliminate the rest to perk up productivity

Day 282

Soaring productivity is drenched in perspiration

Day 283

The belief that one can make a difference can make the difference in productivity

Day 284

Eliminate the unwanted and ineffective movements to uplift productivity

Day 285

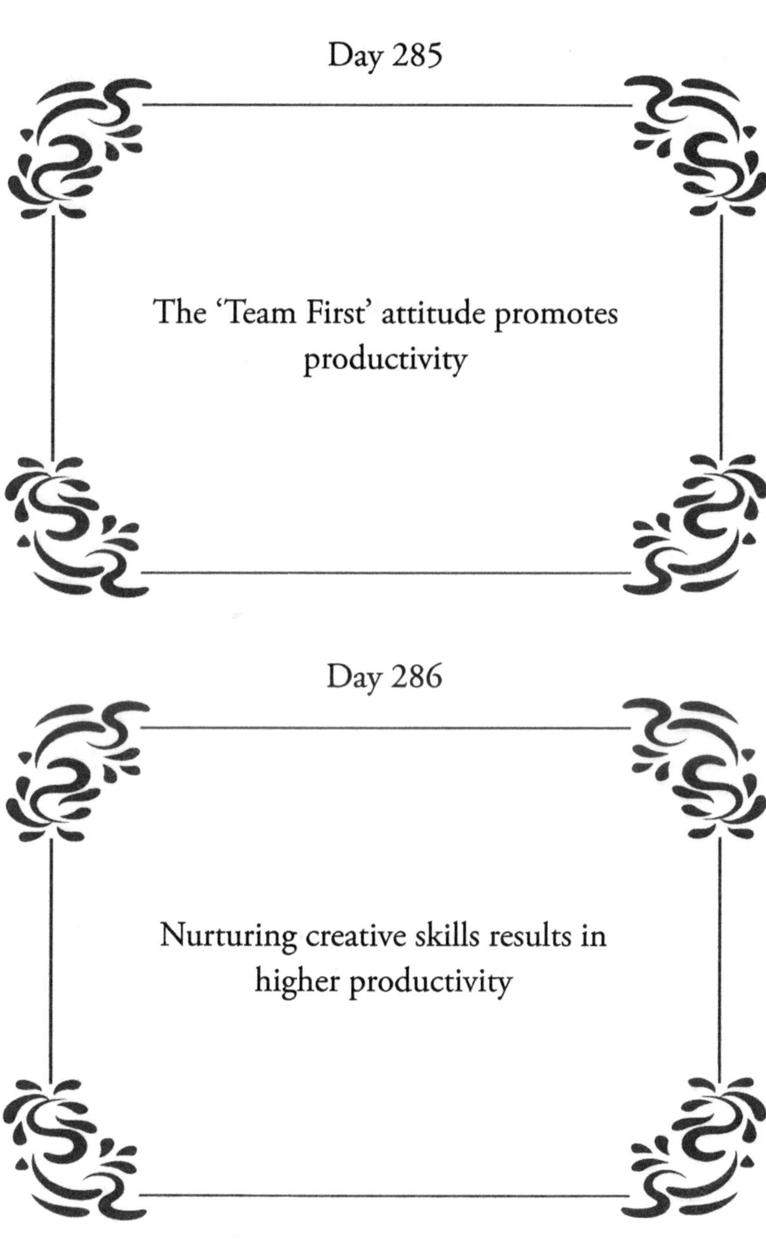

The 'Team First' attitude promotes productivity

Day 286

Nurturing creative skills results in higher productivity

Day 287

Advocate to synergise and champion to sustain productivity

Day 288

Finding fault with others is not helpful to increase productivity

Day 289

Managing time effectively is the key to higher productivity

Day 290

Idleness is the enemy of productivity

Day 291

Killing time kills productivity too

Day 292

Right tools, right methods and right attitude guarantee higher productivity

Day 293

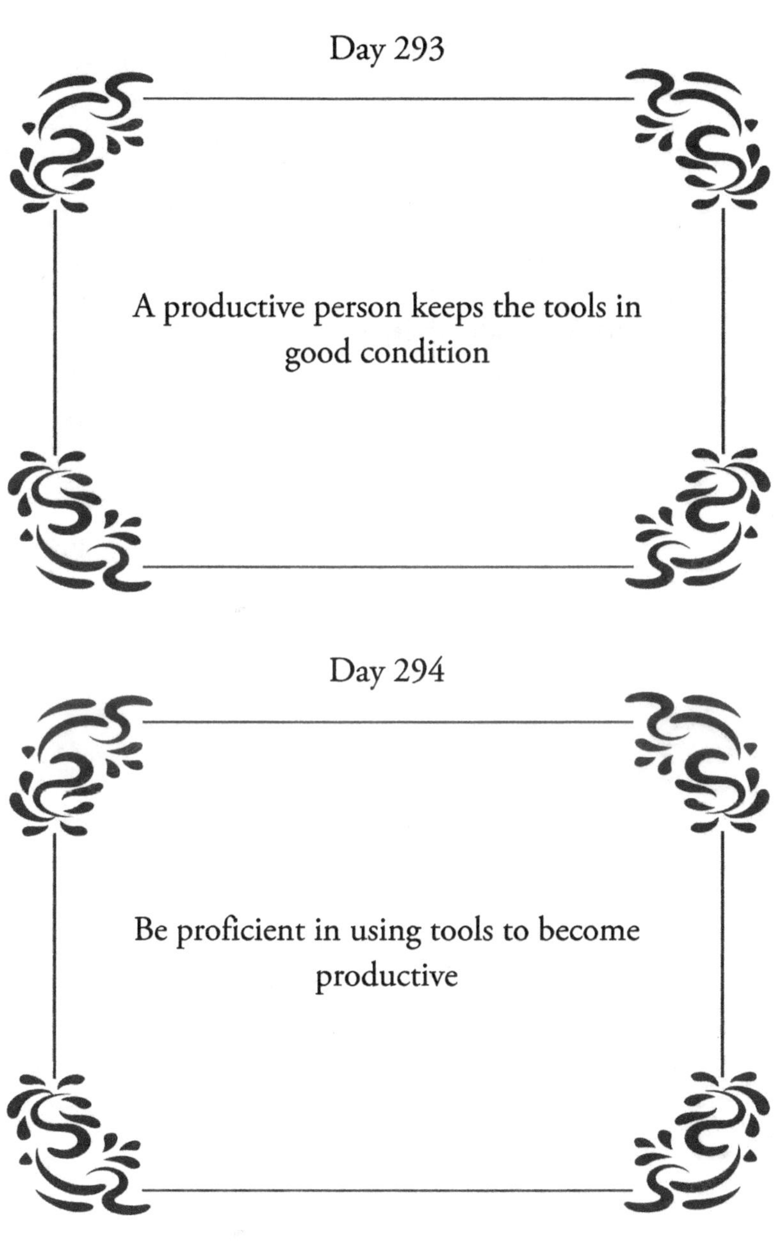

A productive person keeps the tools in good condition

Day 294

Be proficient in using tools to become productive

Day 295

Make productivity the first priority

Day 296

Will power to fight pessimism
helps one in the productivity pursuit

Day 297

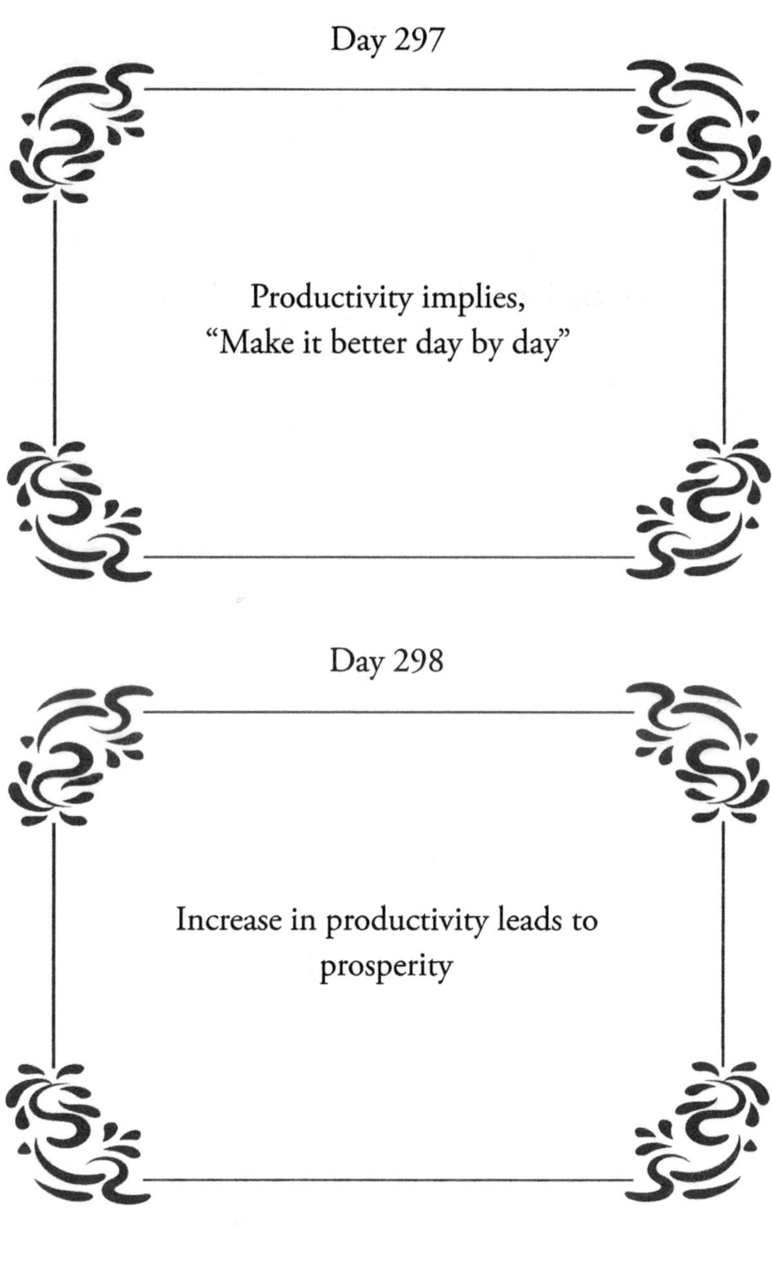

Productivity implies,
"Make it better day by day"

Day 298

Increase in productivity leads to prosperity

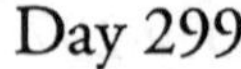

Day 299

Discipline makes the journey to higher productivity effortless

Day 300

A productive leader breeds more productive leaders

Day 301

Be receptive to changes to become productive

Day 302

Nurturing productivity results in higher competitiveness

Day 303

Work-Life balance helps sustain productivity

Day 304

Aesthetic workplace boosts productivity

Day 305

Refine your habits to improve productivity

Day 306

Translating knowledge to action results in productivity

Day 307

KISS (Keep It Simple Stupid)
to promote productivity

Day 308

Say 'no' to unproductive jobs to
increase productivity

Day 309

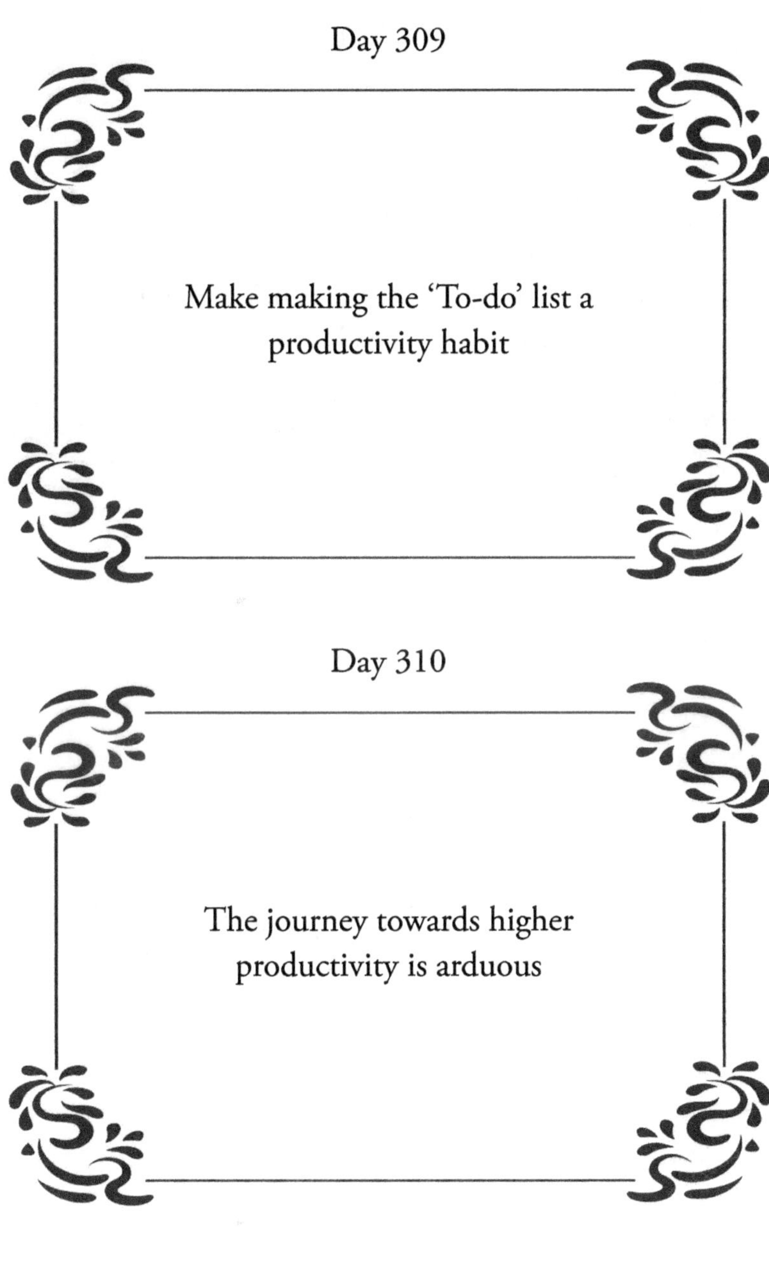

Make making the 'To-do' list a productivity habit

Day 310

The journey towards higher productivity is arduous

Day 311

Holding meetings alone is not enough to increase productivity

Day 312

Higher productivity results from 'using time', not by 'spending it'

Day 313

Aim to increase the productivity not activities

Day 314

Degrees won't help one to increase productivity, skills will

Day 315

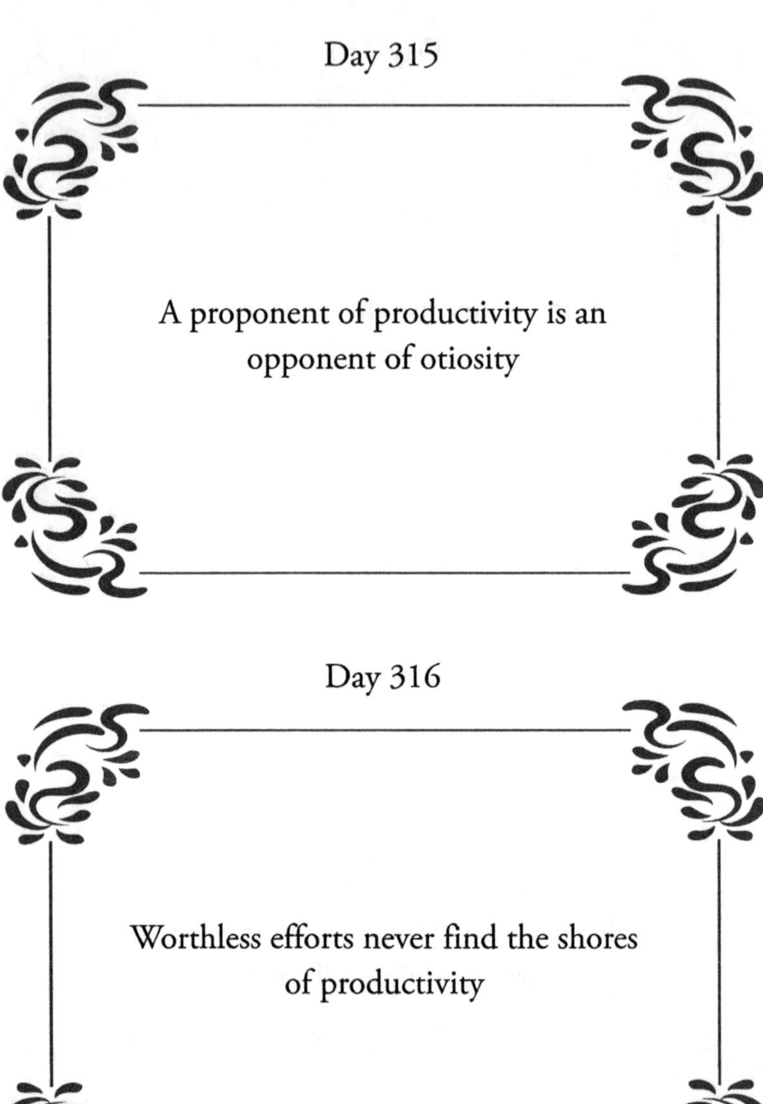

A proponent of productivity is an opponent of otiosity

Day 316

Worthless efforts never find the shores of productivity

Day 317

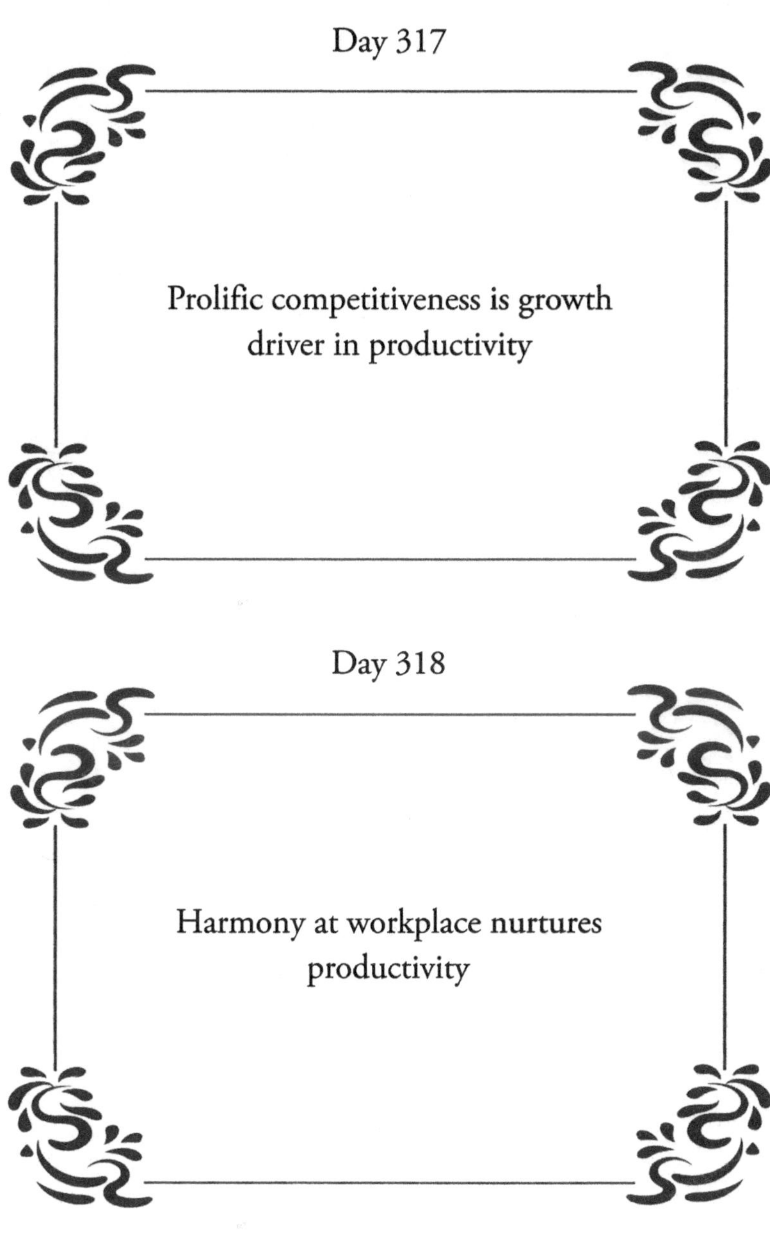

Prolific competitiveness is growth driver in productivity

Day 318

Harmony at workplace nurtures productivity

Day 319

Wellness of employees promotes productivity

Day 320

Be within the agenda to make the meetings productive

Day 321

Avoid fatigue and burnout to remain productive

Day 322

Recharge your batteries to sustain productivity

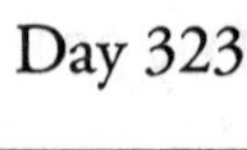
Day 323

Why not use your commute time productively

Day 324

Standardizing tools and methods increase productivity

Day 325

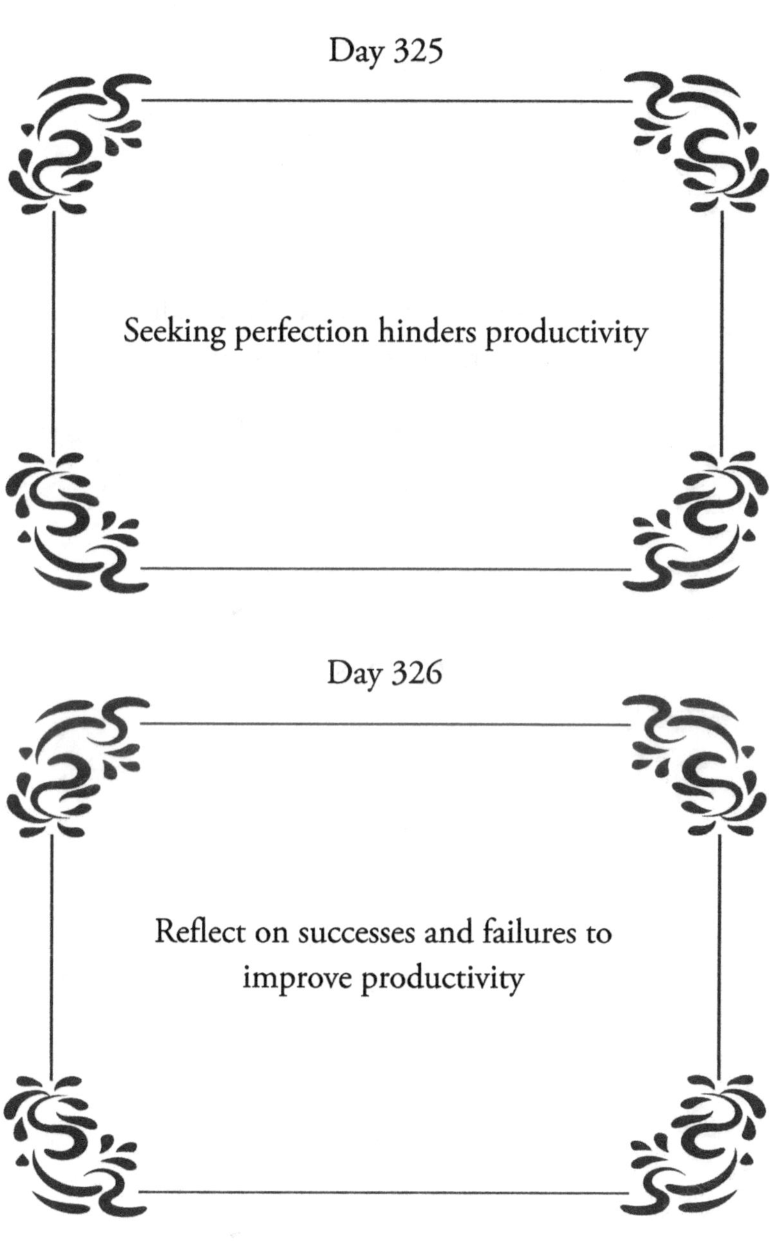

Seeking perfection hinders productivity

Day 326

Reflect on successes and failures to improve productivity

Day 327

Automation of repetitive and low value tasks enhance productivity

Day 328

Productivity is all about eliminating the excessives

Day 329

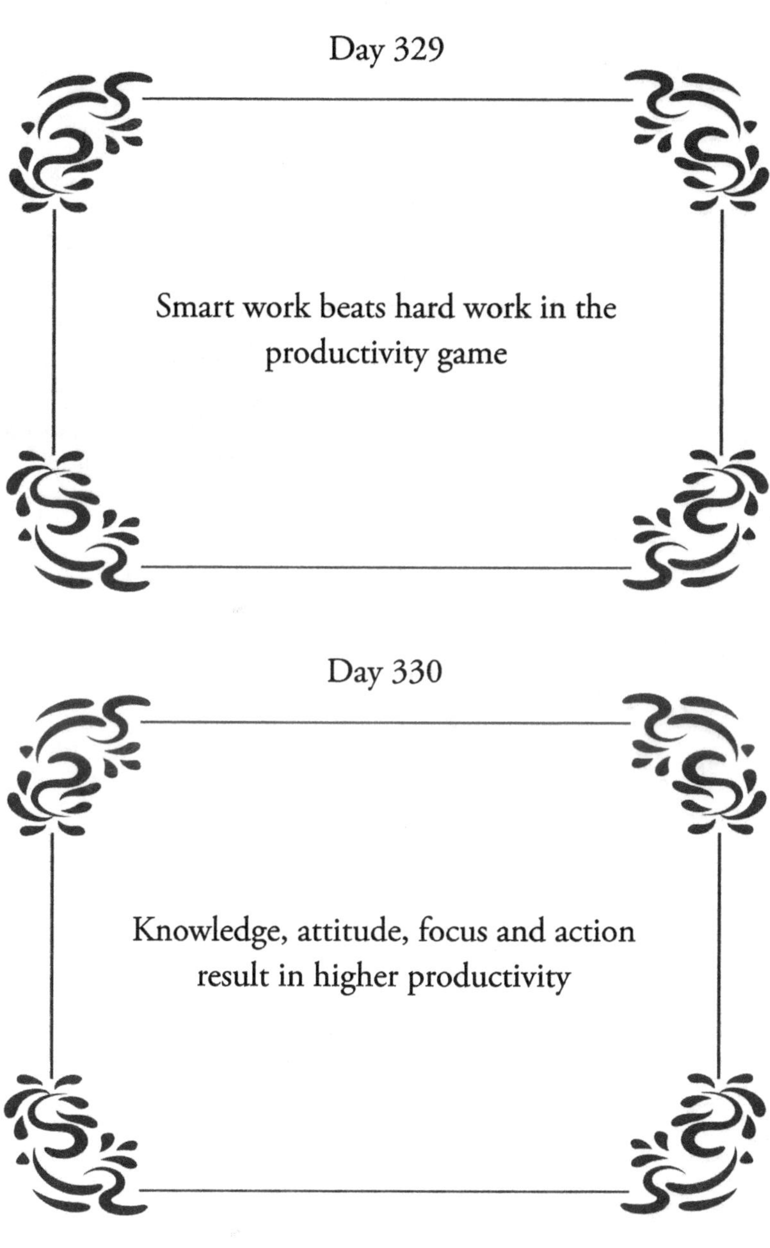

Smart work beats hard work in the productivity game

Day 330

Knowledge, attitude, focus and action result in higher productivity

Day 331

For higher productivity, it is not enough to work only when you feel good

Day 332

Knowledge of productivity is futile until applied

Day 333

Being productive is more important than being busy

Day 334

A simple hard worker is way better than a genius who doesn't work

Day 335

Acknowledging a job well done works wonders in boosting productivity

Day 336

Productivity helps you to stay on course in a chaotic world

Day 337

Never sideline the 'Important' for 'Urgent' when you seek higher productivity

Day 338

Be proactive than reactive to become productive

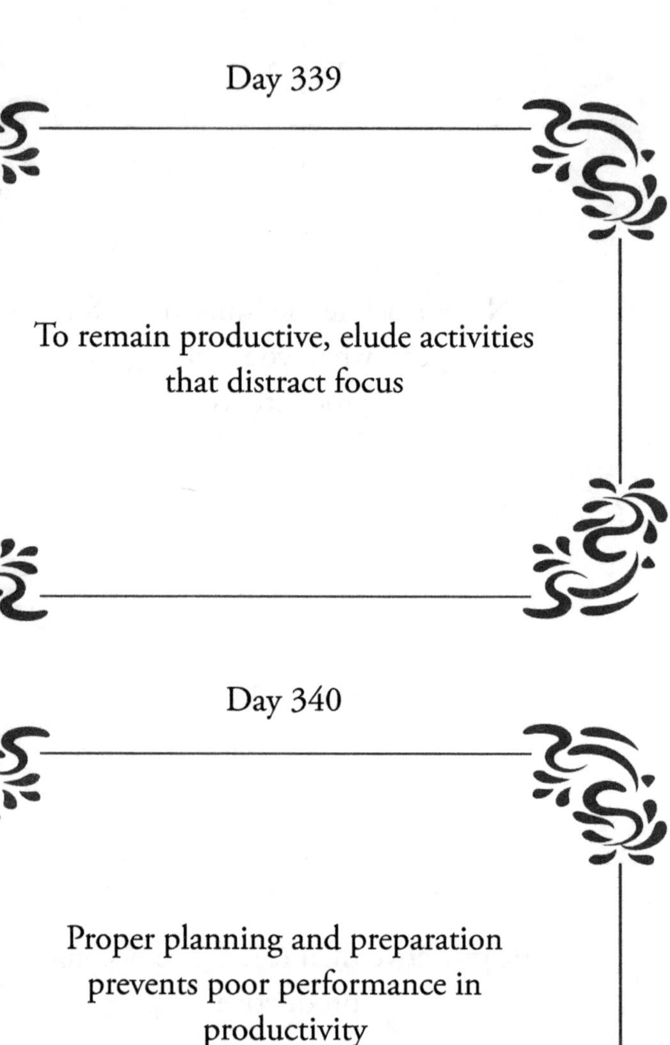

Day 339

To remain productive, elude activities that distract focus

Day 340

Proper planning and preparation prevents poor performance in productivity

Day 341

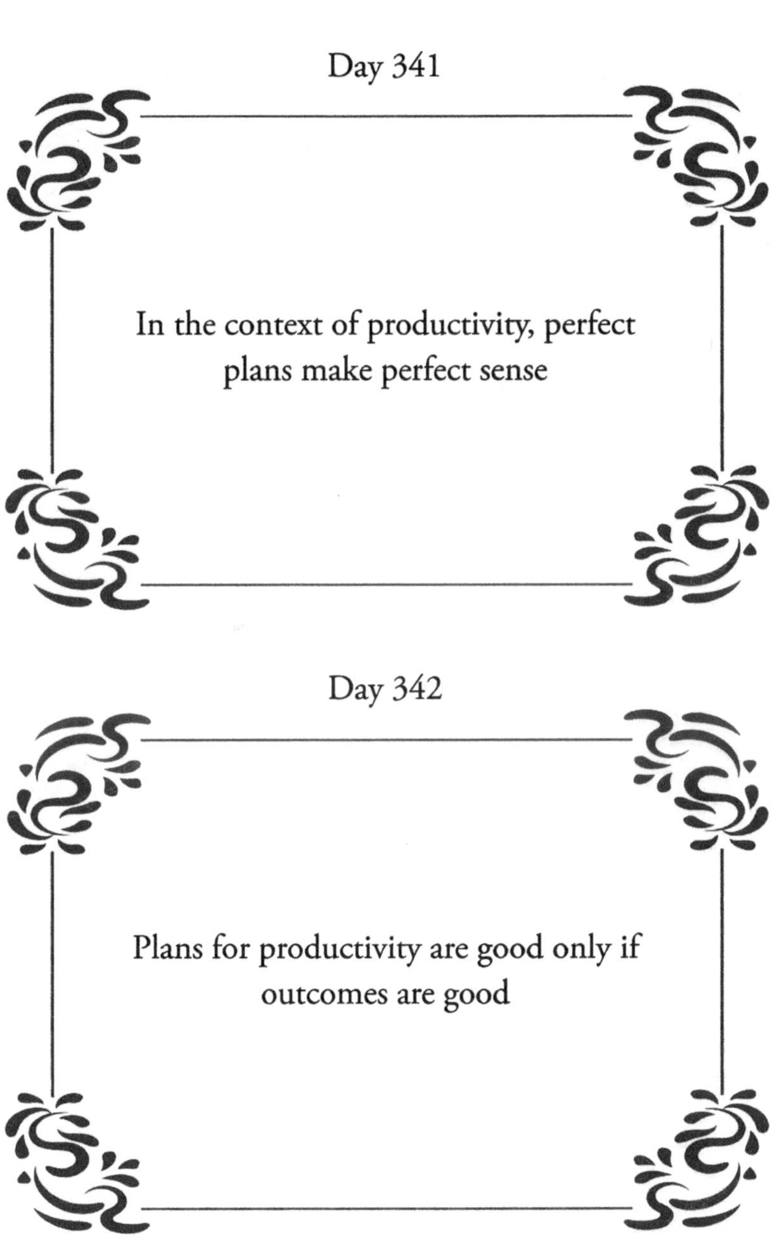

In the context of productivity, perfect plans make perfect sense

Day 342

Plans for productivity are good only if outcomes are good

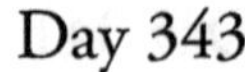

Day 343

Higher productivity is a result of consistency in action

Day 344

Engaging in best time utilization is embracing productivity

Day 345

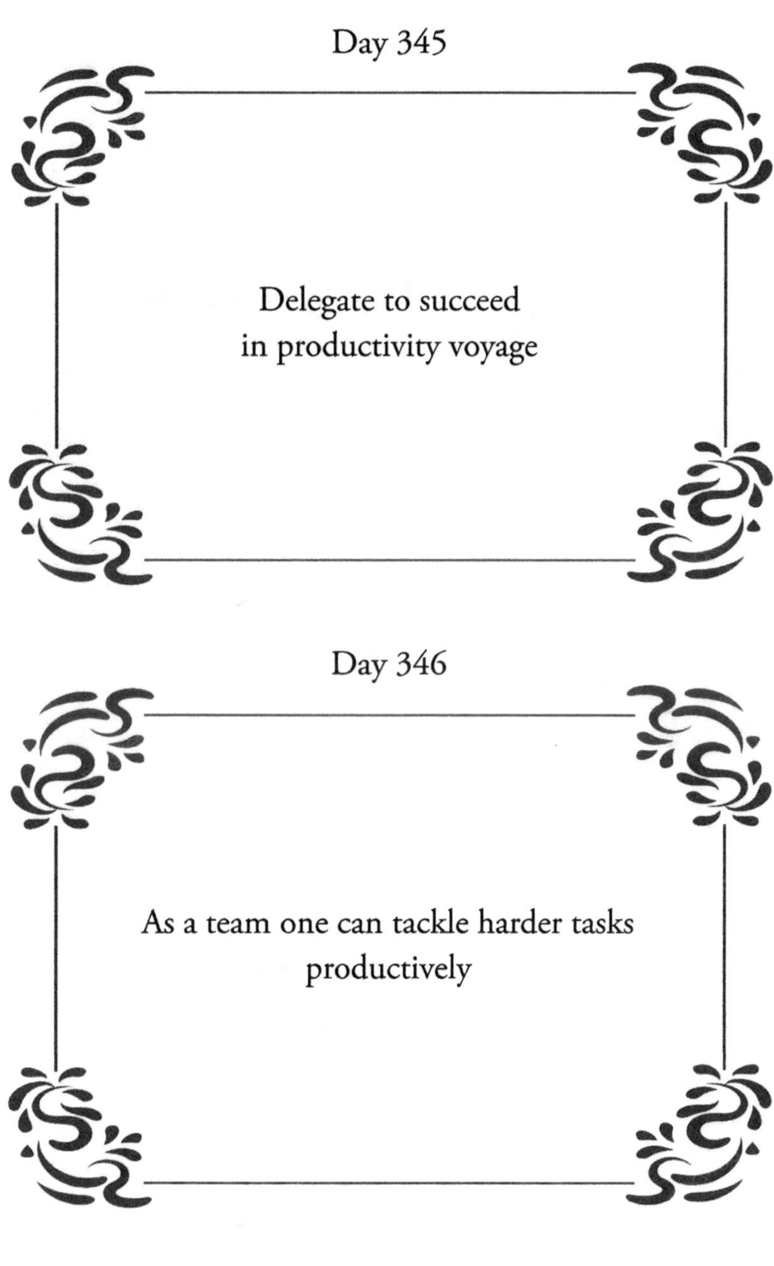

Delegate to succeed
in productivity voyage

Day 346

As a team one can tackle harder tasks
productively

Day 347

Planning and making right choices is also a productive engagement

Day 348

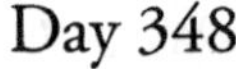

Standardization of tools and methods help boost productivity

Day 349

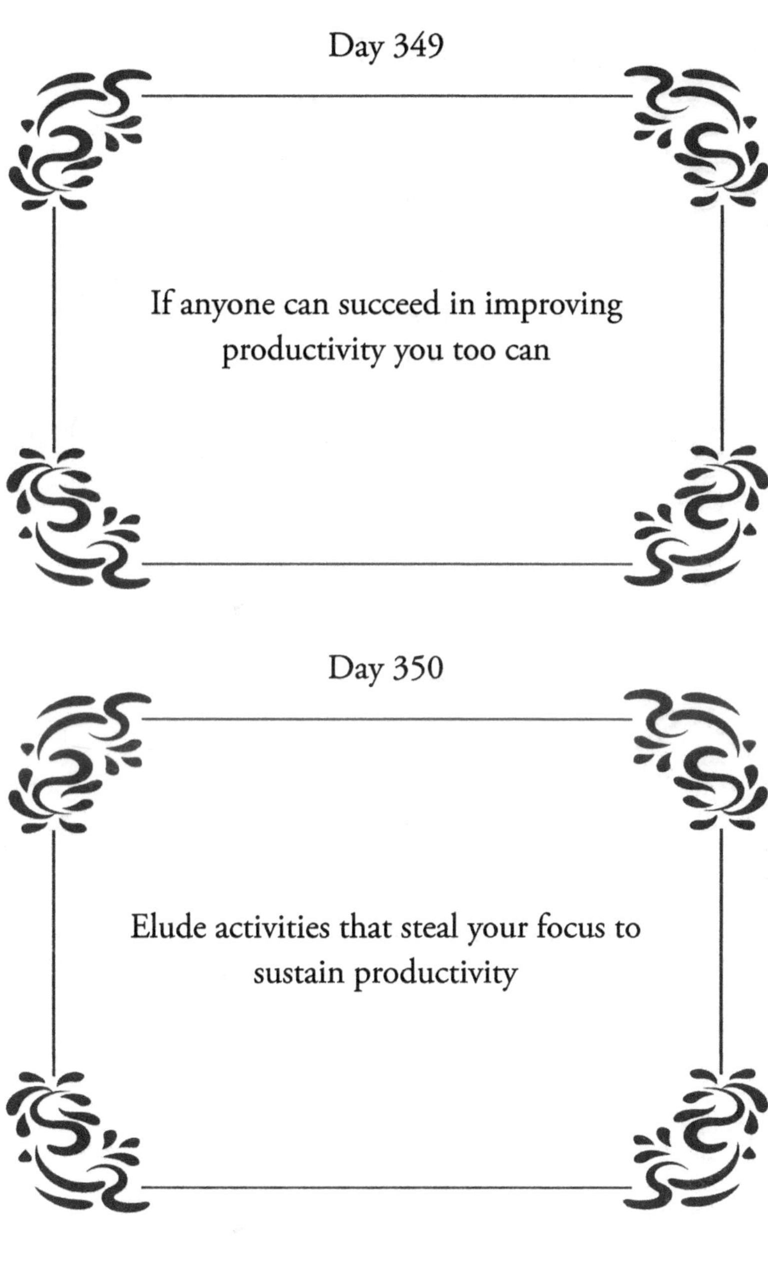

If anyone can succeed in improving productivity you too can

Day 350

Elude activities that steal your focus to sustain productivity

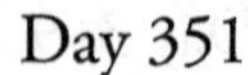

Day 351

Syndicate to spread productivity and sustainability

Day 352

Everyone and every step matters in the ride to higher productivity

Day 353

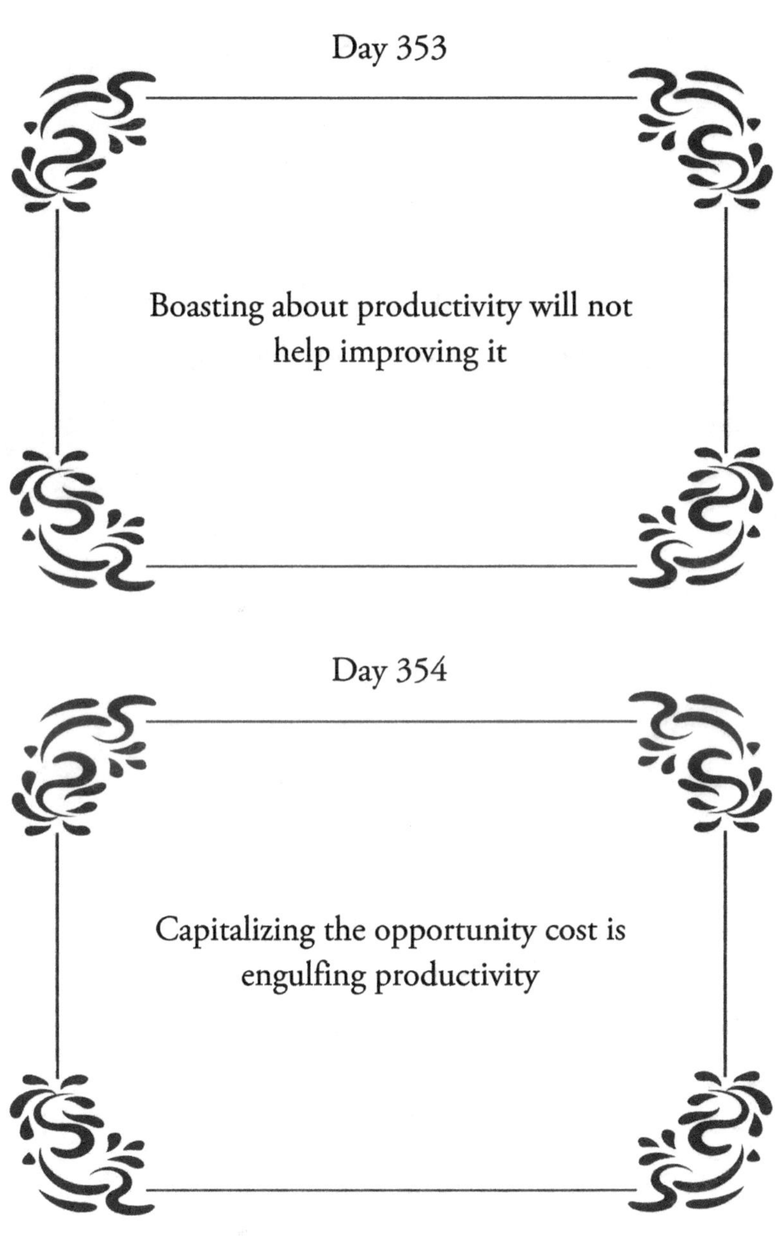

Boasting about productivity will not help improving it

Day 354

Capitalizing the opportunity cost is engulfing productivity

Day 355

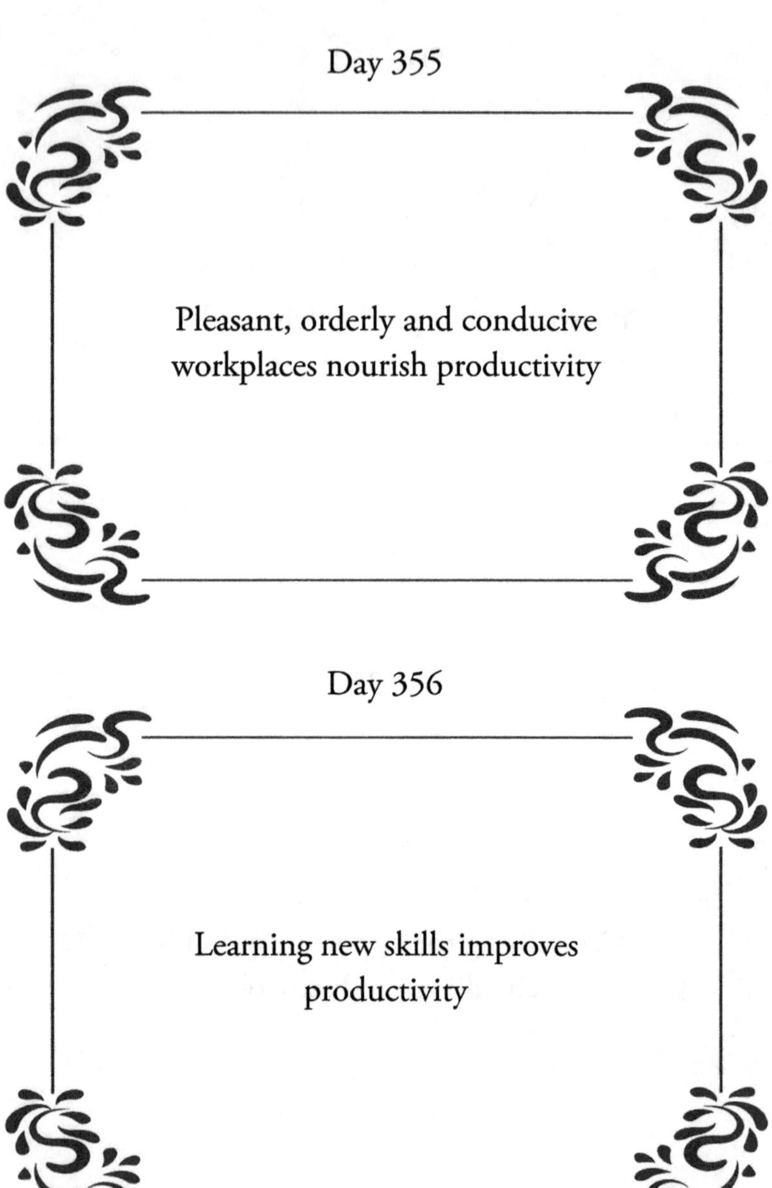

Pleasant, orderly and conducive workplaces nourish productivity

Day 356

Learning new skills improves productivity

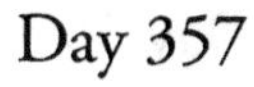

Day 357

Action is better than inaction when it concerns productivity

Day 358

Productivity count on smart work and good time management

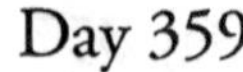

Day 359

Smart phone addiction
leads to drop in productivity

Day 360

Those who learn to apply the learnings
win the productivity race

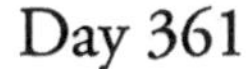

Day 361

Reduction in the search time is a sign of higher productivity

Day 362

Successful people became successful by using their time productively

Day 363

Productivity
strives to empty the emptiness

Day 364

There is no right or wrong way to seek
higher productivity

Day 365

Reward yourself on successes, it pays in the journey of productivity

AUTHORS

Dr Nidhi M B

A graduate of Mechanical Engineering (Production stream) of University of Kerala, she had her post-graduation in Industrial Engineering from College of Engineering Trivandrum and PhD from National Institute of Technology Calicut. She has more than 20 years of experience in Teaching, Research, Industry, Consultancy and Administration. Presently she is Associate Professor at Mar Baselios College of Engineering and Technology, Trivandrum and working as Consultant to K-DISC. She is very active in professional society activities and currently National Executive Council member of ISTE. Nidhi has won the Best Engineering College Teacher award, Best Faculty advisor to students from ISTE Kerala Section and Special appreciation awards for her substantial contributions in the field of Industrial Engineering from IIIE. Nidhi is a much sought after resource person in various training programmes, seminars and International conferences. She also published her collection of poems in the book titled 'Musings' recently and has few funded projects, 50 plus publications to her credit. Her expert talks and publication details are available at http://nidhiscorner.webs.com

Dr Anil Brahmanandan

A graduate of College of Engineering Trivandrum, he had his MTech and PhD from IIT Madras. He has contributed extensively in academics and worked in various engineering colleges in Kerala. He retired as Principal from Government Engineering College Barton hill, Trivandrum. A person known as an institution builder, his contributions can be seen in the development of institutions such as Government Engineering Colleges at Wayanad and Bartonhill, Centre for Engineering Research and Development and TrEST Research Park. He was Director of Kerala State Science and Technology Museum. He is a consultant to various government departments and industry. Anil is a recipient of VKM John Award for best Engineering College Teacher from Indian Society for Technical Education, and special appreciation awards from ISTE and IIIE. An avid advocate of productivity, he has won special mention on three occasions in the National Productivity Competition. He is active in a number of professional bodies and fellow of IE(I), IIIE and AeSI.

Dr K Gopalakrishnan Nair

A graduate from College of Engineering Trivandrum, he had his MTech from IIT Delhi and PhD from Cochin University of Science and Technology. He has worked in academics in various engineering colleges in Kerala and retired as Principal of Government Engineering College Kozhikode. He is responsible for the starting of B.Tech and MTech programmes in Industrial Engineering in University of Kerala and developing the Industrial Engineering group in College of Engineering Trivandrum. The MBA programmes (both Regular and Evening) at College of Engineering Trivandrum are a result of his relentless efforts. He is very active in Indian Institution of Industrial Engineering(IIIE) and helped to grow the institution in various capacities at chapter and National levels. He is a recipient of many awards including the prestigious Lilian Gilbreth award of IIIE for lifetime contribution to Industrial Engineering.

ACKNOWLEDGEMENT

The authors are influenced by the discourses of prominent leaders of management, quality, productivity and other domains. These pioneers became successful by practicing what they preached and also propagating their observations through books and publications. These veterans motivated an entire generation by their deeds and words. We place on record our gratitude to them for inspiring us to consolidate the 365 Productivity sutras. Albert Einstein, Amelia Earhart, Benjamin E Mays, Brian Tracy, Dan S Kennedy, David Allen, Edgar Allan Poe, Dhirubai Ambani, Franz Kafka, Jack Ma, Jonathan Sacks, Henry David Thoreau, Henry Ford, Lao Tzu, Muhammad Ali, N R Narayana Moorthi, Oprah Winfrey, Pablo Picasso, Peter Drucker, Ratan Tata, Robin S. Sharma, Stephen Hawking, Stephen King, Steve Jobs, Tim Ferris, Tony Robbins, Theodore Roosevelt, Tom Peters, Walt Disney, Warren Buffet,,.and many more are in the list. We wish that their teachings motivate the generations to come to strive for excellence.

Authors

ACKNOWLEDGEMENTS

The authors were influenced by many [illegible] and programs [illegible] quality [illegible] and other [illegible] [illegible]

[illegible] Joseph [illegible] Ken [illegible] Tim Ferris, Tony Robbins, [illegible] Peters, [illegible] and [illegible] who are [illegible] the list. We [illegible] their teaching and [illegible] inspirations [illegible]

Authors

www.ingramcontent.com/pod-product-compliance
Lightning Source LLC
La Vergne TN
LVHW050542160826
845677LV00011B/2147

9798887330273